ONE-ACT
COMEDIES
of MOLIÈRE

THE ACTOR'S MOLIÈRE

Translated by Albert Bermel
from Applause Books

THE ACTOR'S MOLIÈRE
VOLUME IV

ONE-ACT COMEDIES of MOLIÈRE

Translated,
and with an introduction,

by
ALBERT BERMEL

Third Edition

APPLAUSE
THEATRE BOOKS

FOR JOYCE

Library of Congress Cataloging-in-Publication Data
Molière, 1622-1673.
    [Selections. English. 1992]
      One-act comedies of Molière / translated, and with an introduction
        by Albert Bermel. -- 3rd ed.
      p. cm. -- (The Actor's Molière ; v. 4)
    Reprint. Originally published: New York : Ungar, 1975.
    ISBN 1-55783-109-2 : $8.95
    1. Molière, 1622-1673--Translations into English. 2. French drama
(Comedy)--Translations into English. I. Bermel, Albert. II. Title. III.
Series: Molière, 1622-1673. Actor's Molière ; v. 4.
PQ1825.E5B4 1992
842'.4--dc20

APPLAUSE THEATRE BOOKS
211 West 71st Street
New York, New York 10023
(212) 496-7511, FAX: (212)721-2856

ACKNOWLEDGMENTS

I am Grateful to Eric Bentley and Lionel Abel, who read and commented on *The Forced Marriage* and *The Imaginary Cuckold* respectively; Mr. Bentley commissioned the translation of *The Forced Marriage* for *The Tulane Drama Review*. *Two Precious Maidens Ridiculed* first appeared in print in the Molière issue of *Drama Critique*. My thanks, too, to the college, high school, and professional theater companies who have staged the plays and written to me about their productions. One of my greatest satisfactions as a translator was to sit in on rehearsals and finished performances of *The Imaginary Cuckold* done by The Theater of the Deaf.

CONTENTS

Fears into Laughs

Molière's longer plays have often unsettled critics who like to keep their genres clean and uncomplicated. *The Misanthrope, Tartuffe, The School for Wives, George Dandin, Don Juan, The Miser,* and *The Learned Ladies* are richly comic yet they contain scenes that are disturbing, if not distressing, to sit through, and they end by stirring up in us a discord of emotions. The genre merchants will not be defeated, though. They have found an answer, a general repository for Molière's drama, the tragicomedy. If redefining the plays in this way helps to keep alive the human quality of Molière's characters, and to kill off the stilted, grimacing, artificial performance, that would-be reconstruction of British "style", then the tragicomic assumption does serve a theatrical purpose. But the dangers of categorizing persist.

There is not an overall balance in Molière between comedy and tragedy, for the tragic sense and effects are partially concealed. My own impression, after watching many Molière productions, is that the glints of bitterness and darkness register better on an audience when the actors do not seem to push for them. If the productions are not funny, very funny, they are not worth doing. Roger Planchon's peerless *Tartuffe,* for example, was greeted by continuous open bursts of laughter; the audience felt uneasy *while* it was enjoying itself. George Saintsbury called Molière "the Master of the Laugh,"[1] but there is more than one kind of laugh. Lionel Abel has written that Molière "lifted comedy to a level of artistry and refinement it had never had before nor has had since"[2]; and John Palmer emphasizes the variety of Molière's comedy when he says that "no man has more finely smiled or more broadly laughed." For the comic actor,

---

[1] The authors and books referred to here are listed in the bibliography, except where otherwise stated.

[2] *Metatheatre* (New York: Hill & Wang, Inc., 1963), p. 64.

I

then, Molière's full-length plays provide not only rewarding roles, but tests of intelligence, sincerity, and versatility. Can the same be said of the one-acts? It can insofar as many of their situations and characters prefigure the ones in the longer plays, or in some instances, duplicate them. Even into the most rollicking of his short plays Molière manages to slip hints and glimpses of somber thoughts and feelings, as we shall see.

But what stands out in these less ambitious works is their twofold comedy, a balance, sometimes a clash, between formal and informal entertainment. On the one side we find a colloquial, rough quality —humor—which proceeds from characters who do not mean to look and sound funny; on the other side we find studied, polished wit that enables other characters to be funny by intention. (Some characters, of course, are both humorous and witty.) The humor, especially the naturalness of its language, was inspired by Molière's years as a traveling performer and enhanced by his knack for clothing dialogue in sentences that appear suspiciously ordinary and uncalculated. The formal wit has mixed origins; it comes partly from the strained, literary mannerisms of seventeenth-century France, partly from his responses to the Court spectators in the mature period of his career, and partly from his striving for new, elevated comic forms.

Molière's training as actor and author began during fifteen years on the road while he circulated among provincial audiences, appearing on a converted tennis court in Agen or Fontenaye,[3] in the consular palace at Narbonne, or in the city halls of Lyon, Nantes, and other large towns. His early sketches and plays, worked up from commedia dell'arte skits of the Italian troupes who visited France frequently in the early seventeenth century, were shot through with popular sight gags, jokes (*burli*), and stage buffoonery (*lazzi*). Like the commedia scenarios they were populated by traditional and familiar figures: the pedant, the cuckold, the tightfisted father, the scheming servants, the aching lovers, the Pistol-like soldier-braggart who refuses to fight. The matter of these entertainments was not altogether primitive and the staging fairly elaborate. Molière's company wore splendid costumes and, in spite of the hasty preparations and a certain helping of improvisation, the actors performed with finesse. The troupe's provincial patrons, such as the Prince de Conti and the Duc d'Epernon, may have enjoyed the boisterous bits of business—

---

[3] The tennis courts did not have makeshift stages, as has sometimes been suggested; they were transformed into serviceable playhouses.

stage beatings, pratfalls, and raw jokes—but must also have expected some subtlety in the writing and presentation. Only two of these early efforts survive, *The Jealous Husband* and *The Flying Doctor;* into them Molière had already begun to infuse literary distinction. He adapted the situations from who knows how many sources, not only from the commedia routines, but also from Plautus and Terence (he is said to have known Terence's work by heart in Latin), and from unnumbered sixteenth- and seventeenth-century dramatists in Spain, France, and Italy. The knockabout humor of these playlets exploited such satisfying, vintage themes as the triumphs of love over greed, youth over age, and honesty over pretence. Later Molière was to investigate these themes more rigorously and, in his longer plays, to present avaricious, aging, and pretentious characters with a combined severity and understanding that have never been surpassed.

In the transitions from early to late plays another theatrical element persisted. It has affinities with folk art because it predates the commedia dell'arte and goes back to wandering performers of the middle ages. It also has affinities with improvisation because it consists of set pieces or bravura turns done by specialized players and by nobody else, so that the author adapts his scripts to the solos done by certain "masks," that is, actors in character. Each of these turns might be compared with an aria used over and over, with negligible variations, in different operas. A succession of such arias—a doctor's followed by an outraged father's and a betrayed lover's—added up to a revue format linked by a flimsy thread of story. The format, obtrusive in the one-act plays, becomes disguised after Molière tremendously strengthens the story line for his large, complex dramas, but it is very much there. The big speeches of Alceste, Acaste, Don Juan, Philaminte, Dandin, Orgon, Tartuffe, and Sosie, superb as monologues, retain the flavor of those solo comic acts. So do the recurring scenes, such as the one in which a maidservant mocks her master (in, say, *The Middle-Class Nobleman*); there must have been a maid's-laughing-and-giggling act which one of the women in the Molière company excelled in, and he made room for it. Some critics have been disappointed that in his very late play *Scapin* Molière returned to commedia scenes, characters, and *lazzi;* the truth is that he had never abandoned them.

Yet we should not underestimate Molière's contributions to the solo turns. The Scholar's long speeches in *The Jealous Husband* and the Lawyer's puffy address to Sganarelle in *The Flying Doctor* have obviously been painstakingly planned and composed, even if they were drawn from existing material. The formal side of Molière's writing thus shows up in these first two of his plays and may have done in such lost plays as *The Woodcutter* and *Gorgibus in the Sack*. In the next two plays the literary notes resound strikingly. *Two Precious Maidens Ridiculed* takes literature as one of its dominant themes and enters the fringes of Parisian high society; while *The Imaginary Cuckold* is written in rhyming verse. In the former play he was not tilling new ground, for there had been at least two previous plays about the *précieuses* of Paris; but in this play Molière acquired what we recognize today as his own satirical tone, probably because the dialogue is based on his personal experiences. In a play written by one of his enemies, a character calls Molière "a dangerous man . . . he goes nowhere without his eyes and ears." He had visited the fashionable Blue Room in the *hôtel* (mansion) of Mme de Rambouillet, dedicated nearly forty years before to cultural discussions, and its imitation, the salon of Mlle de Scudéry on the rue de Beauce, where *précieuses* and their admirers sat in alcoves and buried one another in verbal bouquets. In reproducing their grotesquely sententious exchanges, Molière did not forget to add a generous ration of lowbrow comedy, as when Mascarille makes his entry into the play in a sedan and tries to bully the porters out of their payments, or when he and his fellow valet are thrashed at the end by their masters and forced to strip down in public. The contrast between formality and informality in this play is dramatized when the author juxtaposes the affectations of the girls and the valets with the spontaneous speech patterns of the father, the suitors, and the maid.

By the time he came to write *The Imaginary Cuckold* in 1660 he had tried his hand at verse drama in two five-act comedies, *The Bungler*, 1655, and *The Loving Quarrel*, 1656, and had developed a rhythmic style that was not merely supple enough to accommodate the comedy but actually helped to point it up by skillful use of rhyme, meter, and ictus.

Molière practiced his art at a time when *esprit* (meaning both wit and intelligence) and "correct" form were prized as artistic ends and enforced, if not legislated, by the French Academy. Tragedy was looked up to as literature's summit. Molière performed a number of tragic roles and kept a stock of other authors' tragedies in his repertory. Yet he apparently was unconvincing in serious roles. He could turn his gifts to superb account in mimicry and comedy, but contemporary reports say he lacked the measured, ringing voice that tragic acting then required. If you can't beat the game and don't want to join it, invent your own. One theory has it that Molière's desire to cast comedy in poetic forms may have had something to do with his incapacity as a tragedian; by lifting the standards of comedy he might be able to bring it on a par with tragedy. But no artist sets out to create art that is *equal* to other art. Molière, I surmise, tried to demonstrate that finely wrought comedy can throw surprising light on a potentially tragic situation. It is easy to say with twentieth-century hindsight—or by foreseeing the past, as Paulhan has it—that Molière was bound to succeed in this lofty enterprise. Boileau had told him that his most rollicking speech was "often worth a learned sermon," but it must have been difficult at that time for anybody, Molière included, to be sure that "serious" comedy was a feasible objective; then, suddenly, here was *The Imaginary Cuckold*, its formal and informal constituents in near equilibrium: a farce in poetry.[4] Coming from somebody else the hybrid might have worn the features of a monster; from Molière it proved to be a dramatic innovation. In addition, it proved a success, but Molière's rivals did not acknowledge its qualities any more than they subsequently admired the full-length plays in verse.

The remaining three plays in this book are also weddings of opposites. *The Rehearsal at Versailles* contains a heartfelt exposition of some of Molière's beliefs as a playwright and methods as an actor, but the disruptive sequences—the niggling questions of La Thorillière and the clamor of the courtiers—are quickfire comedy. *The Forced Marriage* pits a dimwitted bourgeois against longwinded scholars and sham nobility until he gives up all hope, a stranger lost in exotic vocabularies. And *The Seductive Countess* is *Two Precious Maidens Ridiculed* translated into a provincial setting where the heroine's sentiments sound even more out of place.

Together these plays represent seven of Molière's ten one-act plays. The other three are omitted for different reasons. *The Criticism of the School for Wives* was born of the controversy that followed the early productions of *The School for Wives* and becomes an orphan

---

[4] The topic of Molière as *farceur* is discussed in Gustave Lanson's essay, and by the director Jacques Copeau (see bibliography).

when separated from the parent play. *Pastorale Comique,* a slight divertissement, was addressed to Louis XIV's vanity. *The Sicilian,* a longer, more substantial divertissement, depends for many of its effects on colossal machinery; some recently built college theatres have vastly more sophisticated plant and equipment than was needed for the original production at Saint-Germain-en-Laye and could handle this comedy-ballet with dispatch, but, as the old stage saw goes, it doesn't read as well as it probably plays. The remaining seven comedies can fairly be called the cream of Molière's one-acts, and in their diversity are not unrepresentative of his work as a whole, even if they never touch the emotional and dialectical sublimity of *Don Juan, Tartuffe, The Misanthrope,* and *The School for Wives.*

In addition to the ten one-acts, Molière wrote two two-acts, nine three-acts, and twelve five-acts; from this diversity we assume that he was aware of the importance of unfolding an action at the right length and with the right strength. In this respect his one-act comedies are models; they run their courses without forcing the speed; they put on a nice dash just before the end, and stop before they are winded or simply moving forward mechanically. A one-act play makes an especially memorable impression when it arises from a single situation; Molière hews scrupulously to this discipline; he enriches the situation with humorous twists and embellishments brought about by the presence of rogues and their marks, fools, but he does not stray too far off the main track. By codifying and at the same time renewing a number of theatrical conventions, Molière realized a new kind of brief comedy, compact, organized, and peopled with figures who stand for quickly recognizable clusters of attributes.

Since the playwright's death in 1673 the growing Molière industry has ground out dozens of editions and interpretations of his drama; the card files are overflowing, and periodicals such as the *Moliériste,* published for a decade during the last century, have devoted themselves to keeping up with new information and criticism. Because not much is known of Molière's first thirty-six years, stray documents about the birth of his wife or the death of his mistress's mother, Marie Hervé, have been pored over for clues, and Molière's life and writings reexamined in the light of the new data, however trifling. Molière as man, author, and performer has undergone many evaluations, and it is not possible (or desirable) to be dogmatic about him or the meanings of his work.

A casual reading of his plays and prefaces suggests that he abhorred extreme behavior, pleading for a sane, middle course in human activity. Accordingly, certain earlier critics and biographers, like Brunetière, formulated a Moliéresque "philosophy" that images him forth as an insufferably wise old advice-donor. "He possessed a quality," says Voltaire, "that sets him apart from Corneille, Racine, Boileau, and La Fontaine: he was a philosopher in theory *and* practice." This remark from one of the shrewdest commentators on human affairs and literature can easily be misinterpreted, and often has been. It is true that a sense of conventional morality, a belief in the powers of common sense and common decency and moderation, does appear to inform the plays. Let us suppose, for the sake of the argument, that Molière was trying to promote moderation among his contemporaries. What is moderation? Surely it involves the suppression of personal whims, mannerisms, and irrational impulses; it calls for an adherence to social norms. We thus have a portrait of Molière as *un homme moyen raisonnable;* his reasonable characters become his mouthpieces, his villains and fools his targets; we then take him (if we are reasonable ourselves and follow the argument through) to be *the* playwright of conformity, as the Goncourt brothers did.[5]

Such a conclusion is at odds with the spirit of the plays themselves. It may be going too far to say that Molière sides with his villains and fools, but it is fair to notice that the extreme characters like Harpagon the miser, Orgon the outrageously jealous host of Tartuffe, Arnolphe the selfish, tormented guardian, and Alceste, the self-appointed conscience of mankind are the backbones of the plays they appear in, and Molière may well have felt a certain affection for them, otherwise he would not have looked into them so piercingly or been able to make them so amuse and worry us. Nor would he have been able to play them, as he did, with such conviction. On the other hand, the sensible figures who plead for natural behavior do not hold leading roles. They are neither as colorful nor as appealing as the villains and fools. They could almost be transplanted, like the scenes in the early comedies, from one play to another. It is hard to imagine that they were not conceived for the sake of dramatic opposition and to give each comedy's fantastic branchings-out roots in the real world.

From the plays to the author. Palmer remarks that "nothing is

[5] *Pages from the Goncourt Journal,* ed. and trans. by Robert Baldick (New York: Oxford University Press, 1962), p. 49.

more dangerous or misleading than to look for an author in his works," and the same might be said of searching for the meaning of an author's works in his life. Not that the life and works tell us nothing about each other; rather, one offers only wispy clues to the other. The transmutation of experience into art encompasses distortions we have no way of assessing. What, for instance, are we to make of Molière's middle-class background from studying the comedies? By piecing together isolated sentences and sentiments we can decide that he detested what Bernard Shaw calls middle-class morality *and* that he thought it the basis for a life of contentment;[6] that he rebelled against his father *and* respected him. We can discover that he "really" loved his wife and that he "really" hated her. We can psychologize at a distance and say with Ramón Fernández that Molière releases his private vexations through his extreme characters and then balances his drama with the commonsensical characters who represent the thoughtful, deliberative side of his personality. Such observations remove us from the plays; they whisk us speculatively on a tour of the author's corpse. Which keeps its silence.

It seems to me a tortuous procedure to apply Molière's plays to his life only in order to refer deductions about his life back again to the plays. We are liable to miss the sharpness and specificity of Molière's actual portraits. If we study the bigger portraits one at a time we notice that most of them have lineaments in common, despite the generous differences in their outward features. Behind the comic words and gestures, palpitated by obsessive behavior patterns— Jourdain's extravagance, Harpagon's avarice, the (dissimilar) snobbery of Alceste, Dandin, and Philaminte, the possessiveness of Orgon and Arnolphe—there lurk fears. Fears of going unheeded, unrecognized, unloved. Each of these characters wants to be master (or mistress) of a household, a metaphor for being in control of oneself, able to hold up to the world an acceptable image of oneself. The fears and their consequences are hilarious to watch, but terrifying for the characters to undergo because they spring from desperation; the plays, instead of allaying those fears, make them come true. In Molière's funniest moments we are never far from nightmare, the inexorable acting out of the worst that could happen. It is not that events exactly get out of control; rather, the more the characters

---

[6] Molière was Shaw's favorite playwright. See Archibald Henderson, *George Bernard Shaw: Man of the Century* (New York: Appleton-Century-Crofts, 1956), p. 502.

try to exert control the more they bring to pass what they most dread. Arnolphe finally *is* a cuckold; Dandin makes *and publicly shows* himself inferior to his wife; Alceste, in his rejection of Célimène, turns out to be no better than other people in the Parisian *haut monde* whom he despises. These characters are born losers. We laugh; they do not. Dandin says *"Marchand qui perd ne peut rire"* —the loser cannot laugh. With a few exceptions, these characters fear being unloved because they are unable to give love or, indeed, much else.[7] They have little or nothing to give, and that is what they receive. They have made their empty beds and must lie in them.

Now, we do not need to conclude that Molière is handing out practical advice to the lovelorn—give of your affection and ye shall receive. He would surely be among the first to understand that such advice is fruitless, like instructing a dog how to behave like a cat. He saw in his time people, perhaps including himself, who strove to cope with their fears in ways that could only aggravate those fears and ultimately realize them. Neither in the long plays nor the short ones do I see any implicit remedies. But why should one expect remedies? A playwright has no obligation to turn healer; in Molière healers are all quacks. Like the Greeks and Shakespeare before him, like his acquaintances Corneille and Racine, like Ibsen and Pirandello and Chekhov after him,[8] Molière analyzed life and clothed his analysis in theatrical forms that have allowed his vision to live more vividly than his contemporaries' prosaic reports.

A contributor to *The Oxford Companion to the Theatre* believes that Molière's plays are "universal in their application, yet untranslatable. In transit, the wit evaporates and only a skeleton plot is left. This, however, will not deter people from trying to translate them—a fascinating preoccupation." It is true that Molière, who made many enemies during his lifetime, has all too often since his death needed protection from his translating friends. But Richard Wilbur's versions of *The Misanthrope, Tartuffe*, and *The School for*

---

[7] The exceptions include Monsieur Jourdain and Argan, whose escapades end fairly happily, and also Don Juan and Amphitryon, who are special cases that I hope to discuss at more length elsewhere.

[8] In *Men and Masks* (see bibliography) Lionel Gossman devotes a detailed chapter called "After Molière" (pp. 252-306) to the effects of Molière's "unflinching honesty" on later European writers.

Wives, and Tony Harrison's modernized *The Misanthrope,* set in the time of De Gaulle, all follow the French devotedly without sacrificing style and simplicity in their English verse. This book has a more modest objective: to bring the vernacular side of the short comedies into play. Up-to-the-minute slang is not the answer; in addition to dating too rapidly, it wrenches the plays out of their period and environment. But nor does it help to take the sentences practically word for word from the French, as some translators have done, finishing up with a computerized English that makes the plays sound like Restoration comedies composed by an illiterate.

Ten years ago when the first edition of these translations was published I started to enunciate some principles of translating Molière into a language that is actable. Today I think that literary principles, when offered by a translator as by an author, are useless excuses, apologies, self-justification. All that matters is results. A translator works by instinct. He has to trust his ear, his senses. He is lucky or unlucky. But his luck is more likely to hold as long as he feels unabated respect and love for the plays in their original form.

Albert Bermel

Herbert H. Lehman College, 1975

LES PRECIEUSES RIDICULES

This engraving, done by Brissart for the publication in 1682 of Molière's plays, was probably taken from a sketch made during a performance of *Two Precious Maidens Ridiculed*. In the scene represented here the extravagantly dressed valets, Mascarille and Jodelet, exchange effusive greetings (see p. 62), while the young *précieuses*, Magdelon and Cathos, look on with pride at having, as they believe, attracted to their house a pair of leading courtiers. By some fluke of inverse perspective—or with the aid of unusually high heels—the girls appear much taller than the men. In the background the wall panel with its view of a mountain lake suggests that the performance took place privately in one of the royal apartments.

The Jealous Husband

As a curtain raiser, *La Jalousie du Barbouillé* may have been performed scores of times during Molière's itinerant years in the provinces, from 1645 to 1658. It contains the remnants of a commedia dell'arte scenario based, in turn, on a tale by Boccaccio. The manuscript was discovered in 1731 in the possession of a poet named J.-B. Rousseau. Molière had probably formalized it as a text at some point in its career, after it had undergone many transformations. An entire scene between Le Barbouillé and his wife was later moved, with minor changes, into a longer play, *George Dandin or The Outwitted Husband.* In that play too the husband knows that his wife is trying to pull something on him, if not succeeding, but he cannot do anything about it except protest and be called a fool and a drunkard for his pains. The less-than-angelic wife is named Angélique in both plays. The servants who were to occupy such large roles in later plays hardly appear in *The Jealous Husband;* the impudent companion-maid Cathau shows Le Barbouillé an unkind tongue once or twice, but the burden of the plot is carried by the tormented hero and the Scholar. Like all Molière's early plays this one was performed in masks—or sometimes, more simply, flour and blackening as makeup—which allowed the actor little or no recourse to facial expression and put the emphasis on his voice and movements. The play sweeps along merrily enough, but, like its successor, *The Flying Doctor,* is kissed off with an all too perfunctory closing line. Here directors may want to add a dance or a ceremonial exit, as was probably done in the original stagings.

THE JEALOUS HUSBAND

La Jalousie du Barbouillé

CHARACTERS:

LE BARBOUILLÉ, the jealous husband
ANGÉLIQUE, his wife
GORGIBUS, her father
VALÈRE, in love with Angélique
CATHAU, Angélique's chaperone
THE SCHOLAR
VILLEBREQUIN, brother of Gorgibus
LA VALLÉE, friend of Valère

Scene: [*A peaceful, empty street on the outskirts of Paris. The three houses that are visible belong to* LE BORBOUILLÉ, *his father-in-law,* GORGIBUS, *and the* SCHOLAR.]

[LE BARBOUILLÉ *runs out of his house.*]

BARBOUILLÉ: This I admit: I'm the unluckiest husband in the world. My wife does whatever she can to anger me. Instead of comforting me and obeying my wishes, she drives me out of my mind twenty times a day. Instead of taking care of the house she likes skipping out for walks, living the high life, and mixing with the worst sort of people. — Poor Barbouillé! You're so miserable. But you must punish her. What if you killed her? — No, that's a feeble suggestion; they'd hang me for it. — Put her in prison? — No, the hussy would get hold of a skeleton key and break out. — But you must do something to make her suffer. — Stop arguing. Here comes my learned neighbor; I'll ask him for some ideas.

[*The* SCHOLAR *is strolling by, but stops when* LE BARBOUILLÉ *hails him.*]

Monsieur, I was coming to look for you, to ask you about a matter of some importance.

SCHOLAR: My dear Barbouillé, you are badly brought up, unlettered, and ill-mannered to accost me without raising your hat and without considering the time, the place, or the person you are addressing. How dare you begin to speak to me in hasty, unprepared language? You should preface your words with, "Good health to you, Doctor, you most learned of doctors." What do you take me for, my good man?

BARBOUILLÉ: Excuse me, my head was in a whirl. I wasn't thinking of what I was doing. But I realize that you're a fine fellow.

SCHOLAR: Do you know where that *fellow* comes from?

BARBOUILLÉ: I couldn't care less, so help me, if he comes from Marseilles or Manchuria.

SCHOLAR: The word *fellow* breaks down into two component syllables, *fell* and *low*, which have nothing to do with falling to the ground but are derived from the medieval words *feo* and *laga*, meaning *fee* and *lay*, respectively. That is, he who lays down a fee is offering himself as a partner, therefore he is to be trusted, hence he is a *fellow*.[1]

BARBOUILLÉ: I think I fellow—follow. So much for that. Now, Monsieur, I want to talk to you about——

SCHOLAR: You utter that word *Monsieur* as though I were a mere gentleman.

BARBOUILLÉ: What else are you?

SCHOLAR: A doctor. Nay, more—I am one, two, three, four, five, six, seven, eight, nine, and ten times a doctor:

[*holding up one finger*] First, just as the unit is the prime integer, the foundation, and the first among numbers, so I am the first among doctors, the doctor of doctors.

[*holding up two fingers*] Second, just as those twin faculties, sense and understanding, are necessary for the complete apprehension of all matters, so I, who am all sense and all understanding, must be twice a doctor.

BARBOUILLÉ: Fair enough. Still——

[1] In French Molière plays with the word *gallant,* which he derives from *élégant.*

SCHOLAR: [*holding up three fingers*] Third, just as three is the perfect number, according to Aristotle, so I and all my works are perfect; therefore, I am thrice a doctor.

BARBOUILLÉ: Now, wait a minute——

SCHOLAR: [*holding up four fingers*] Fourth, just as philosophy is divided into four parts—logic, morals, physics, and metaphysics—so I am totally conversant with all four and thus four times a doctor.

BARBOUILLÉ: Who's denying it? Listen, will you——

SCHOLAR: [*holding up five fingers*] Fifth, just as there are five universal categories—genus, specimen, difference, rule, and exception—without which it is impossible to reason correctly, so I, a master of reasoning, am five times a doctor.

BARBOUILLÉ: For all I care, you could be a horse doctor.

SCHOLAR: [*holding up six fingers*] Sixth, just as six is the number of working days in the week, so I, who work unceasingly to further my fame, am six times a doctor.

BARBOUILLÉ: Keep talking. I'm not listening.

> [*From now until the* SCHOLAR *finishes his speech,* LE BARBOUILLÉ *makes all kinds of unsuccessful efforts to contain his rage.*]

SCHOLAR: [*holding up seven fingers*] Seventh, just as seven represents felicity, so I, who am acquainted with all the means of achieving happiness, an acquaintance for which I thank my bountiful talents—so I, let me repeat, am obliged to say of myself: "Oh, three plus four times happy doctor."

[*holding up eight fingers*] Eighth, just as eight stands for justice, because of the equality between the fours, of which there are two, and the twos, of which there are four, so I, who can boast of the justice and prudence with which I weigh and measure all my actions, am eight times a doctor.

[*holding up nine fingers*] Ninth, just as there are nine Muses, so I am equally adored by them all.

[*holding up ten fingers*] Tenth, whereas, when you come to this number you cannot exceed it without repeating the other numbers, and whereas it is the universal number, therefore—therefore I say, when you come to me you cannot exceed me, for you have come to the universal doctor: I include all other doctors.

And so you see by plausible, true, demonstrated, and convincing reasons that I am one, two, three, four, five, six, seven, eight, nine, and ten times a doctor.

BARBOUILLÉ: What the devil was all that? I thought I'd met a wise man who could give me some sensible advice, and all I've found is an idiot who babbles and counts his fingers. One, two, three, four, five, six— Ha! Ha, ha! Ha, ha, ha! Ha, ha, ha, ha! And so on. Let me say one thing: I'm not asking you to waste your time and I'm not looking for free advice. If you give me satisfaction I'll give you what you want. You want a fee? A fee you shall have. Money, understand?

SCHOLAR: Money, eh?

BARBOUILLÉ: You're darn right, money. And whatever else you ask for.

SCHOLAR: [*swinging his cloak around him*] So! you take me for a man who would do anything for money, a usurer, is that it? Let me tell you, my friend, that if you gave me a purse crammed with gold coins, and that purse in an inlaid box, and that box in a precious casket, and that casket in a priceless coffer, and that coffer in a rare cabinet, and that cabinet in a magnificent room, and that room in the luxurious wing of a sumptuous castle, and that castle part of an incomparable citadel, and that citadel the pride of a great city, and that city the capital of a fertile county, and that county belonging to a wealthy province, and that province set in a flourishing kingdom, and that kingdom the most powerful in the world— If you gave me *the world itself,* or only the flourishing kingdom, or only the wealthy province, or only the fertile county, or only the great city, or only the incomparable citadel, or only the sumptuous castle, or only its luxurious wing, or only the magnificent room, or only the rare cabinet, or only the priceless coffer, or only the precious casket, or only the inlaid box, or only the purse crammed with gold coins, or only one single, but valuable, gold coin—without the purse— I would care as little for your money or for you as [*snapping his finger*] that!

[*He goes off.*]

BARBOUILLÉ: What a slip! He calls himself a doctor, so I thought I'd have to talk money to him. But if he doesn't want any payment I'm only too glad to oblige him. Doctor, come back—

[*He runs off after the* SCHOLAR.]

[ANGÉLIQUE *appears with* CATHAU *and* VALÈRE.]

ANGÉLIQUE: I assure you, Monsieur, that I am grateful for your company. My husband is so ugly, so debauched, and so besotted with drink that it's torture for me to be with him. You can imagine how much satisfaction a girl must get from a grouch like that.

VALÈRE: My dear lady, I am honored by your request, and I promise to do everything I can to entertain you. Since you don't find my company disagreeable, I will try to repay the joy your sweet words have given me with my most sincere attentions.

CATHAU: Psst! Change the subject. Here come some bad tidings in person.

[LE BARBOUILLÉ *returns.*]

VALÈRE: [*raising his voice*] Madame, it grieves me to have to bring you such unfortunate news, but you would have heard it from somebody else if not from me; and as your brother is so ill——

ANGÉLIQUE: Say no more, Monsieur. I thank you for going to this trouble. At your service.

[VALÈRE *bows and leaves.*]

BARBOUILLÉ: [*aside*] Well, well, I don't have to apply to the notary for my cuckold certificate. [*aloud*] So, Madame Trollop, I find you with a man, after all the warnings you've had from me. Now you're trying to plant horns in the furrows of my forehead.

ANGÉLIQUE: Don't lose your reason. The gentleman came to inform me that my brother is ill. Is that something to fight about?

CATHAU: He's back again. Never gives us five minutes of peace.

BARBOUILLÉ: You're a pair of sluts. You, Cathau, you're the one who's corrupting my wife. As soon as she took you on, she started to go downhill.

CATHAU: You're a fine one to talk, with the uphill example you set.

ANGÉLIQUE: Don't bother with him, the drunk. He's so bottled he doesn't know what he's saying.

[GORGIBUS *comes in with* VILLEBREQUIN.]

GORGIBUS: Isn't that my wretched son-in-law quarreling with my daughter again?

VILLEBREQUIN: We'd better see what's wrong.

GORGIBUS: Now what? You're always squabbling. Is there never any peace in your household?

BARBOUILLÉ: The creature called me a drunk. [*to* ANGÉLIQUE] I have a good mind to clout you a stiff one in front of your father.

GORGIBUS: If you do, by God, I'll give up the dowry and take her back.

ANGÉLIQUE: He's the one that always starts.

CATHAU: [*to* GORGIBUS] You put a curse on her when you gave her to this tightwad.

VILLEBREQUIN: Enough, everybody. Quiet, quiet!

[*The* SCHOLAR *comes back.*]

SCHOLAR: What is going on here? Difference of opinion? Disturbance? Dissension? Dispute? Disorder? Disruption? Disintegration? Gentlemen, ladies, please, please! Let us see if there is not some way of reaching a settlement. I hereby appoint myself your peacemaker, in order to promote harmony among you.

GORGIBUS: My daughter and son-in-law are at odds.

SCHOLAR: What sort of odds? Tell me more so that I can even them out.

GORGIBUS: Monsieur——

SCHOLAR: Briefly, please.

GORGIBUS: All right. Keep your bonnet on.

SCHOLAR: Do you know the origin of the word *bonnet?*

GORGIBUS: No.

SCHOLAR: It comes from the Latin words *bonus est,* meaning it is good. Why is it good? you ask.

GORGIBUS: I was just going to——

SCHOLAR: A bonnet is good because it keeps away catarrh and bronchitis.

GORGIBUS: Good God, I didn't know that.

SCHOLAR: Heh. Now, briefly: the cause of the quarrel.

GORGIBUS: Here's what happened——

SCHOLAR: I know that you will not wish to detain me unnecessarily, since I beg you not to. I have urgent business in town. However, if I can bring your family together again, I am willing to stay for one moment.

GORGIBUS: In one moment I can tell you all about it.

SCHOLAR: Be quick, then.

GORGIBUS: Here's how the trouble started——

SCHOLAR: Please remember, Monsieur Gorgibus, that it is a pleasure to hear from a man who can speak his mind in a few words. The great talkers are not intent on forcing other people to listen to them endlessly; often they express themselves so tersely that it is impossible to understand them. *Virtutem primam esse puta compescere linguam*: that is, the greatest virtue is to control one's tongue. The finest quality in a gentleman is to know what *not* to say.

GORGIBUS: In that case, you——

SCHOLAR: Socrates gave his disciples three careful recommendations: "Restrain your behavior, curb your appetite, and shorten your speeches." Now begin, Monsieur Gorgibus.

GORGIBUS: I will if you let me.

SCHOLAR: Slice away all the gibberish, come straight to the point, measure every word, speak to me only in epigrams. Quick, quick, Monsieur Gorgibus, hurry. You're lagging.

GORGIBUS: Will you for God's sake let me say something?

SCHOLAR: Get to it, Monsieur Gorgibus. You're spluttering away and wasting words. Somebody else had better give me the explanation.

VILLEBREQUIN: I will, Monsieur. You realize that——

SCHOLAR: You, Monsieur, are an ignoramus, an antischolar, an enemy of speech, or in simple language, a donkey. What, you begin your narrative without so much as a preamble? I refuse to listen. Will somebody else please speak? You, Madame, let me have some indication of what has happened here.

ANGÉLIQUE: Do you see that fat fool of a husband of mine, that sack of sour wine there?

SCHOLAR: Gently, gently. Speak of your spouse with respect when you stand in the presence of a preeminent scholar.

ANGÉLIQUE: Some doctor you are. I scoff at you, your doctorings, and your doctrines. I can play the doctor too when I want to.

SCHOLAR: You can play—I'm sure you can. You look as if you can play with the parts of speech. You like orgies of talk, conditional words that depend on conjunctions; you like the masculine gender, the genitive case, the preposition that introduces a proposition; you are fond of sin-tactics and strong rhythms and a regular beat. You [*to* LE BARBOUILLÉ], come here; perhaps you can give me a coherent account of the cause of this outbreak.

BARBOUILLÉ: Doctor——

SCHOLAR: At last we are beginning properly. "Doctor"—the word chimes sweetly in my ears, with the right degree of emphasis. Continue.

BARBOUILLÉ: It was my wish——

SCHOLAR: Even better! "It was my wish—" The wish presupposes the will, the will presupposes the means to enforce that will, and by means of the means an end may be attained. And since an end implies an object you could have said nothing more fitting than "It was my wish."

BARBOUILLÉ: I'm boiling——

SCHOLAR: Strike out that word "boiling." It is coarse and vulgar.

BARBOUILLÉ: Will you listen to me, for pity's sake?

SCHOLAR: "Listen to me, *audi quaeso*," the words of Horace.[2]

BARBOUILLÉ: There've been enough horrors already today. If you don't shut up and listen to me I'll break your doctoring head.

> [*At this point everybody begins to speak at once:* LE BARBOUILLÉ, GORGIBUS, VILLE-BREQUIN, ANGÉLIQUE, *and* CATHAU. *The* SCHOLAR *enumerates his reasons why peace is a desirable objective. At this point* LE BARBOUILLÉ *seizes his leg and throws him over on his back. While he is down,* LE BARBOUILLÉ *ties a piece of cord around his ankles and drags him off. Traveling on his*

2 Actually, those of Cicero, with whose name Molière plays (*Ciceron, si se rompt*).

back, the SCHOLAR *continues to count off reasons on his fingers (the actor playing this part can ad lib his lines, only snatches of which are audible) until he disappears.*]

GORGIBUS: Villebrequin, we must leave. Go back into the house, daughter, and learn to live with your husband.

VILLEBREQUIN: Good day to you, ladies.

[*They go out;* ANGÉLIQUE *retires into the house with* CATHAU.]

[VALÈRE *crosses the stage with his friend* LA VALLÉE.]

VALÈRE: I am grateful to you, La Vallée, for making the appointment, and I promise to be there in one hour.

LA VALLÉE: You can't alter the arrangement. If you arrive only fifteen minutes late the party will be over and you'll miss seeing the lady you love. You'd better come with me immediately.

VALÈRE: Very well.

[*They go off.*]

[ANGÈLIQUE *comes cautiously out of the house again.*]

ANGÉLIQUE: Seeing that my husband isn't about, I'll slip out to this party one of my neighbors is giving. I'll be back before he will, because he's sitting in some bar. He'll never realize that I set foot outside. The heartless brute leaves me on my own in the house, as if I were his dog.

[*She steals away.*]

[*The stage lighting begins to dim as* LE BARBOUILLÉ *returns, rubbing his hands.*]

BARBOUILLÉ: I knew I'd get the better of that pedant. Ignorant I may be, but I brought him and his theories down to earth. Now I'll go indoors and see what my little wife has prepared for dinner.

[*He goes inside.*]

[ANGÉLIQUE *comes back.*]

ANGÉLIQUE: I was unlucky; arrived there too late. The party was over and the last people were leaving when I walked in. Never mind; the appointment with Valère will keep until next time. I'll go back indoors as if nothing had happened. What's this? The door is locked. Cathau, Cathau!

BARBOUILLÉ: [*leaning out of the window*] Cathau, Cathau! Ha, ha. What is she up to? And how about you, you trash, where have you come from at this time of the night, in this weather?

ANGÉLIQUE: Open up, let me in, and I'll tell you afterward.

BARBOUILLÉ: You can go back where you came from and sleep there. Or in the gutter, if you prefer that. I'm not letting any street-walker into my house. I never heard of such a thing—going out alone at this hour. I don't know if I'm imagining it, but my forehead feels as if it's breaking out.

ANGÉLIQUE: Why are you complaining that I'm on my own? You shout at me when I have company. What am I supposed to do?

BARBOUILLÉ: You're supposed to stay in the house and prepare my dinner and sweep up and look after the children. But I'm not wasting any more words on you. Good-bye, good night. Go to the devil and let me go to bed.

ANGÉLIQUE: You won't open the door for me?

BARBOUILLÉ: No I won't.

ANGÉLIQUE: Please, my darling, I beg of you. Open up, my sweet, and let me in.

BARBOUILLÉ: Crocodile! Serpent! Your honeyed words drip with treachery.

ANGÉLIQUE: Let me come in, please.

BARBOUILLÉ: Never. Get thee behind me, Satan.

ANGÉLIQUE: Then you absolutely won't let me in?

BARBOUILLÉ: No.

ANGÉLIQUE: You have no pity for the wife who loves you so madly?

BARBOUILLÉ: No, I'm a rock; you've injured me and I'm as incensed as a maniac, in other words, very much. I'm unmovable.

ANGÉLIQUE: If you drive me too far, I'll lose my temper and do something you'll be sorry for.

BARBOUILLÉ: What will you do, my bird?

ANGÉLIQUE: If you don't open this door right away, I'll kill myself in front of it. My father always comes past on his way home at night, to see if we're all right. He'll find me lying here. And you'll be hung.

BARBOUILLÉ: That's a good one. Who'll be worse off? I get rid of my wife, while you lose your life. Besides, you'd never do a thing like that.

ANGÉLIQUE: You don't believe me? Look, I have a knife here, ready. If you don't let me in, I'll plunge it into my heart.

BARBOUILLÉ: Watch out! That blade looks sharp.

ANGÉLIQUE: Will you let me in?

BARBOUILLÉ: I've told you enough times: *No.* Kill yourself. Perish. Go straight to hell. I don't give a damn.

ANGÉLIQUE: Then, farewell—[*pretends to stab herself.*] Ah, I am dying!

BARBOUILLÉ: She'd never be stupid enough to do it. I'd better go down with a candle to make sure.

[*He disappears.*]

ANGÉLIQUE: If I can only slip into the house while you're out here, we'll see who turns the tables.

[LE BARBOUILLÉ *comes out of the door in his nightgown and nightcap, carrying a candlestick and peering about. He steps forward.* ANGÉLIQUE *comes out of the shadow and goes quietly inside, closing the door behind her.*]

BARBOUILLÉ: I knew she wasn't that much of a fool. If she's dead, she died running. Or else a breeze blew her body away. Still, she did frighten me for a moment. Lucky for her she decided to scoot. If I'd found her alive, after giving me a scare like that, I'd have let her feel five or six smart kicks in the rear end. That would've taught her something. Well, I'm going to bed.

[*He turns to go in and finds the door closed.*]

That's funny. The wind must have slammed the door shut. Cathau, open up! Cathau!

ANGÉLIQUE: [*leaning out of the same window*] Cathau, Cathau! Ha, ha. What is she up to? And where have you come from, you drunken slop? Watch out; my father will be coming by any minute now, and he'll know the truth at last. You walking wine-butt, you don't budge from that bar, while your poor wife sits alone with the children and you don't know if we need something, and all the time we're biting our nails and wondering whether you'll ever come home.

BARBOUILLÉ: Let me in, you she-devil, or I'll break you in bits.

[GORGIBUS *comes along with* VILLEBREQUIN.]

GORGIBUS: Now what? Still quarreling?

VILLEBREQUIN: You should have made up by now.

ANGÉLIQUE: Look at him down there, as looped as a figure eight. Imagine: he shows up at this hour and starts to shout in the street. And threatens me.

GORGIBUS: Look here, this is no time to come home. If you were a good family man you'd go to bed at a respectable hour and behave decently to your wife.

BARBOUILLÉ: May I drop dead if I've been out of the house. If you don't believe me, ask those people down in the front row. She's the one who just came home. Oh, innocence, thou art betrayed!

VILLEBREQUIN: Now, now, let's settle everything. Tell her you're sorry.

BARBOUILLÉ: I'll see her in flames first. I'm so mad I can't breathe.

GORGIBUS: Daughter, it's up to you. Kiss your husband and make up.

[ANGÉLIQUE *comes down, gives* LE BAR-
BOUILLÉ *a kiss and a mischievous smile,
both of which he submits to.*]

[*The* SCHOLAR *leans out of his window next door, also
wearing his nightgown.*]

SCHOLAR: Hello! More trembling and twittering? More trouble? More turbulence? More tumult? More turmoil? Now what's the matter? Can't a man get a night's sleep?

VILLEBREQUIN: It's nothing, Doctor. Everybody's at peace.

SCHOLAR: With reference to that word *peace*, would you like me to read you a chapter of Aristotle, in which he proves that all the parts of the universe can coexist only when there is peace between them?

VILLEBREQUIN: Is it a long chapter?

SCHOLAR: Only eighty or ninety pages.

VILLEBREQUIN: Thanks, but we won't keep you up.

GORGIBUS: Some other night, Doctor.

SCHOLAR: You don't want to hear it?

GORGIBUS: No.

SCHOLAR: Then I wish you good night; or in Latin, *bona nox.*

[*He disappears.*]

VILLEBREQUIN: And the rest of us can go out together for dinner.

CURTAIN

The Flying Doctor

The character of Sganarelle first appears in *Le Médecin volant* and his namesake recurs in no fewer than six other plays by Molière, though in different guises: as a servant (*Don Juan*), a fiancé (*The Forced Marriage*), a husband (*The School for Husbands, The Doctor in Spite of Himself,* and *The Imaginary Cuckold*), and a father (*Love, The Doctor*). In introducing the wily serving man into this play, Molière was adapting a personage from commedia dell'arte and also setting a pattern for himself and later authors (Beaumarchais's Figaro, for example), whether the character is called Sganarelle, Mascarille, Sosie, or Scapin. Sganarelle illustrates the dichotomy in Molière's writing referred to in the introduction. He seems like a crudely drawn personality at first; later he proves to have nearly inexhaustible resources of sophistication as he works himself into a sweat, apparently for the sake of his master but actually because he delights in exercising his ingenuity. When he first appears, the spectator wonders whether this simpleton can possibly impersonate a doctor. But surprise! He puts on a corpse-side manner more convincingly than a genuine doctor could. *The Flying Doctor* is a tour-de-force role for a comedian; except for one interlude during which the lawyer takes over, he is in command of the stage for almost the entire play, and the part makes heavy demands on his verbal and physical agility, short though the text may be. Some critics have frowned on the "urine scene," finding it below Molière's usual taste. So much the worse for their sense of humor. Molière evidently relished some of the situations enough to use them again, first in *Love, The Doctor* and again in *The Doctor in Spite of Himself.*

THE FLYING DOCTOR

Le Médecin volant

CHARACTERS:

GORGIBUS, a respectable, comfortable, credulous citizen
LUCILE, his daughter
SABINE, his niece
VALÈRE, young man in love with Lucile
SGANARELLE, valet to Valère
GROS-RENÉ, valet to Gorgibus
A LAWYER

Scene: [*A street in a small French town.*]

[VALÈRE, *a young man, is talking to* SABINE, *a young woman, in front of the house of* GORGIBUS, *her uncle.*]

VALÈRE: Sabine, what do you advise me to do?

SABINE: We'll have to work fast. My uncle is determined to make Lucile marry this rich man, Villebrequin, and he's pushed the preparations so far that the marriage would have taken place today if my cousin were not in love with you. But she is—she has told me so—and since my greedy uncle is forcing our hand, we've come up with a device for putting off the wedding. Lucile is pretending to be ill, and the old man, who'll believe almost anything, has sent me for a doctor. If you have a friend we can trust, I'll take him to my uncle and he can suggest that Lucile is not getting nearly enough fresh air. The old boy will then let her live in the pavilion at the end of our garden, and you can meet her secretly, marry her, and leave my uncle to take out his anger on Villebrequin.

VALÈRE: But where can I find a doctor who will be sympathetic to me and risk his reputation? Frankly, I can't think of a single one.

SABINE: I **was** wondering if you could disguise your valet? It'll **be** easy for him to fool the old man.

VALÈRE: If you knew my valet as I do— He's so dense **he'll** ruin everything. Still, I can't think of anybody else. I'll try to find him.

[SABINE *leaves.*]

Where can I start to look for the halfwit?

[SGANARELLE *comes in, playing intently with a yo-yo.*]

Sganarelle, my dear boy, I'm delighted to see you. I need you for an important assignment. But I don't know what you can do——

SGANARELLE: Don't worry, Master, I can do anything. I can handle any assignment, especially important ones. Give me a difficult job. Ask me to find out what time it is. Or to check on the price of butter at the market. Or to water your horse. You'll soon **see** what I can do.

VALÈRE: This is more complicated. I want you to impersonate **a** doctor.

SGANARELLE. A doctor! You know I'll do anything you want, Master, but when it comes to impersonating a doctor, I couldn't do it if I tried—wouldn't know how to start. I think you're making fun of me.

VALÈRE: If you care to try, I'll give you one hundred francs.

SGANARELLE: One hundred whole francs, just for pretending to be **a** doctor? No, Master, it's impossible. You see I don't have the brains for it. I'm not subtle enough; I'm not even bright. So that's settled. I impersonate a doctor. Where?

VALÈRE: You know Gorgibus? His daughter is lying in there ill— No, it's no use; you'll only confuse matters.

SGANARELLE: I bet I can confuse matters as well as all the doctors in this town put together. Or kill patients as easily. You know the old saying, "After you're dead, the doctor comes." When I take a hand there'll be a new saying: "After the doctor comes, you're dead." Now I think it over, though, it's not that easy to play a doctor. What if something goes wrong?

VALÈRE: What can go wrong? Gorgibus is a simple man, not to say stupid, and you can dazzle him by talking about Hippocrates and Galen. Put on a bold front.

SGANARELLE: In other words, talk about philosophy and mathematics and the like. Leave it to me, Master; if he's a fool, as you say, I think I can swing it. All I need is a doctor's cloak and a few instructions. And also my license to practice, or to put it another way, those hundred francs.

[*They go out together.*]

[GORGIBUS *enters with his fat valet,* GROS-RENÉ.]

GORGIBUS: Hurry away and find a doctor. My daughter's sick. Hurry.

GROS-RENÉ: Hell's bells, the trouble is you're trying to marry her off to an old man when she wants a young man; that's the only thing making her sick. Don't you see any connection between the appetite and the illness.

GORGIBUS: I can see that the illness will delay the wedding. Get a move on.

GROS-RENÉ: All this running about and my stomach's crying out for a new inner lining of food and now I have to wait for it. I need the doctor for myself as much as for your daughter. I'm in a desperate state.

[*He lumbers off.*]

[SABINE *comes in with* SGANARELLE *behind her.*]

SABINE: Uncle, I have good news. I've brought a remarkably skilled doctor with me, a man who has traveled across the world and knows the medical secrets of Asia and Africa. He'll certainly be able to cure Lucile. As luck would have it, somebody pointed him out to me and I knew you'd want to meet him. He's so clever that I wish I were ill myself so that he could cure me.

GORGIBUS: Where is he?

SABINE: Standing right behind me. [*She moves away.*] There he is.

GORGIBUS: Thank you so much for coming, Doctor. I'll take you straight to my daughter, who is unwell. I'm putting all my trust in you.

SGANARELLE: Hippocrates has said—and Galen has confirmed it with many persuasive arguments—that when a girl is not in good health she must be sick. You are right to put your trust in me, for I am the greatest, the most brilliant, the most doctoral physician in the vegetable, mineral, and animal kingdoms.

GORGIBUS: I'm overjoyed to hear it.

SGANARELLE: No ordinary physician am I, no common medico. In my opinion, all others are quacks. I have peculiar talents. I have secrets. *Salamalec* and *shalom aleichem. Nil nisi bonum? Si, Signor. Nein, mein Herr. Para siempre.* But let us begin.

[*He takes* GORGIBUS' *pulse.*]

SABINE: He's not the patient. His daughter is.

SGANARELLE: That is of no consequence. The blood of the parent and the blood of the child are the same. *Si? Nein. Per quanto? Nada.* And by examining the father I can reveal the daughter's malady. Monsieur Gorgibus, is there any way in which I might scrutinize the invalid's urine?

GORGIBUS: Of course. Sabine, hurry. Bring the doctor a sample of Lucile's urine.

[*Sabine goes into the house.*]

Doctor, I'm afraid my daughter may die.

SGANARELLE: Tell her to be careful. She is not supposed to amuse herself doing things like that without a doctor's prescription.

[SABINE *comes out with a beaker full of urine and gives it to* SGANARELLE, *who drinks it.*]

It's very warm. There must be some inflammation in her intestines. Nevertheless, she is not seriously ill.

GORGIBUS: [*gaping*] You swallowed it?

SGANARELLE: Not immediately. I let it wash about in my mouth first. An ordinary doctor would merely look at it, but I am extraordinary. As the liquid touches my taste buds, I can tell both the cause of the illness and its probable development. But this was a meager specimen. I need another bladderful.

SABINE: She had enough trouble getting that much out.

SGANARELLE: I never heard of such reluctance. Tell her she must urinate freely, copiously. As much as she can manage.

SABINE: I'll try.

[*She goes off again into the house. This time we see, through a window, how the "urine" is procured:* SABINE *is holding an-*

other beaker and LUCILE *is pouring white wine into it from a bottle.*]

SGANARELLE: [*licking his beaker, aside*] If every invalid pissed like this I'd stay a doctor for the rest of my life.

[SABINE *returns with the second beaker, a tiny liqueur glass.*]

SABINE: She says this is definitely all she has available. She can't squeeze out another drop.

SGANARELLE: This is scandalous. Monsieur Gorgibus, your daughter will have to learn to do better than this. She's one of the worst urinators I've encountered. I can see that I'll have to prescribe a potion that encourages her to flow more generously. Now, may I see the patient?

SABINE: She may be up by now. I'll bring her out.

[*She goes into the house and brings* LUCILE *back with her.*]

SGANARELLE: How do you do, Mademoiselle? So you are sick?

LUCILE: Yes, Doctor.

SGANARELLE: That is a striking sign that you are not well. Do you feel pains in your head, in your kidneys?

LUCILE: Yes, Doctor.

SGANARELLE: Very good. As one great physician has said in regard to the nature of animal life—well—he said many things. We must attribute this to the interconnections between the humors and the vapors. For example, since melancholy is the natural enemy of joy, and since the bile that spreads through the body makes us turn yellow, and since there is nothing more inimical to good health than sickness, we may conclude with that great man that your daughter is indisposed. Let me write you a prescription.

GORGIBUS: Quick! A table, paper, some ink—

SGANARELLE: Is there anybody here who knows how to write?

GORGIBUS: Don't you?

SGANARELLE: I have so many things to think of I forget half of them. Now it's obvious to me that your daughter needs fresh air and open prospects.

GORGIBUS: We have a very beautiful garden and a pavilion with some rooms that look out on it. If you agree, I can have her stay there.

SGANARELLE: Let us examine this dwelling.

[*They start to go out.*]

[*The* LAWYER *appears.*]

LAWYER: Monsieur Gorgibus—

GORGIBUS: Your servant, Monsieur.

LAWYER: I hear that your daughter is sick. May I offer my services, as a friend of the family?

GORGIBUS: I have the most scholarly doctor you ever met looking into this.

LAWYER: Really? I wonder if I might be able to meet him, however briefly?

[GORGIBUS *beckons to* SGANARELLE. LU-CILE *and* SABINE *have moved offstage.*]

GORGIBUS: Doctor, I would like you to meet one of my dear friends, who is a lawyer and would like the privilege of conversing with you.

SGANARELLE: I wish I could spare the time, Monsieur, but I dare not neglect my patients. Please forgive me.

[*He tries to go. The* LAWYER *holds his sleeve.*]

LAWYER: My friend Gorgibus has intimated, Monsieur, that your learning and abilities are formidable, and I am honored to make your acquaintance. I therefore take the liberty of saluting you in your noble work, and trust that it may resolve itself well. Those who excel in any branch of knowledge are worthy of all praise, but particularly those who practice medicine, not only because of its utility, but because it contains within itself other branches of knowledge, all of which render a perfect familiarity with it almost impossible to achieve. As Hippocrates so well observes in his first aphorism, "Life is short, art is long, opportunity fleeting, experiment perilous, judgment difficult: *Vita brevis, ars vero longa, occasio autem praeceps, experimentum periculosum, judicium difficile.*"

SGANARELLE: [*confidentially to* GORGIBUS] Ficile, bicile, uptus, downtus, inandaboutus, wrigglo, gigolo.

LAWYER: You are not one of those doctors who apply themselves to so-called rational or dogmatic medicine, and I am sure that you conduct your work with unusual success. Experience is the great teacher: *experientia magistra rerum*. The first men who practiced medicine were so esteemed that their daily cures earned them the status of gods on earth. One must not condemn a doctor who does not restore his patients to health, for healing may not be effected by his remedies and wisdom alone. Ovid remarks, "Sometimes the ill is stronger than art and learning combined." Monsieur, I will not detain you longer. I have enjoyed this dialogue and am more impressed than before with your percipience and breadth of knowledge. I take my leave, hoping that I may have the pleasure of conversing with you further at your leisure. I am sure that your time is precious, and . . .

> [*He goes off, walking backwards, still talking, waving good-bye.*]

GORGIBUS: How did he strike you?

SGANARELLE: He's moderately well informed. If I had more time I could engage him in a spirited discussion on some sublime and elevated topic. However, I must go. What is this?

> [GORGIBUS *is tucking some money into his hand.*]

GORGIBUS: Believe me, Doctor, I know how much I owe you.

SGANARELLE: You must be joking, Monsieur Gorgibus. I am no mercenary. [*He takes the money.*] Thank you very much.

> [GORGIBUS *goes off, and* SGANARELLE *drops his doctor's cloak and hat at the edge of the stage, just as* VALÈRE *reappears.*]

VALÈRE: Sganarelle, how did it go? I've been worried. I was looking for you. Did you ruin the plan?

SGANARELLE: Marvel of marvels. I played the part so well that Gorgibus thought I knew what I was talking about—and paid me. I looked at his home and told him that his daughter needed air, and he's moved her into the little house at the far end of his garden. You can visit her at your pleasure.

VALÈRE: You've made me very happy, Sganarelle. I'm going to her now.

[*He rushes away.*]

SGANARELLE: That Gorgibus is a bigger dimwit than I am to let me get away with a trick like that. Save me—here he comes again. I'll have to talk fast.

[GORGIBUS *returns.*]

GORGIBUS: Good morning, Monsieur.

SGANARELLE: Monsieur, you see before you a poor lad in despair. Have you come across a doctor who arrived in town a short while ago and cures people miraculously?

GORGIBUS: Yes, I've met him. He just left my house.

SGANARELLE: I am his brother. We are identical twins and people sometimes take one of us for the other.

GORGIBUS: Heaven help me if I didn't nearly make the same mistake. What is your name?

SGANARELLE: Narcissus, Monsieur, at your service. I should explain that once, when I was in his study, I accidentally knocked over two containers perched on the edge of his table. He flew into such a rage that he threw me out and swore he never wanted to see me again. So here I am now, a poor boy without means or connections.

GORGIBUS: Don't worry; I'll put in a good word for you. I'm a friend of his; I promise to bring you together again. As soon as I see him, I'll speak to him about it.

SGANARELLE: I am very much obliged to you, Monsieur.

[*He goes out and reappears in the cloak and hat, playing the doctor again and talking to himself.*]

When patients refuse to follow their doctor's advice and abandon themselves to debauchery and——

GORGIBUS: Doctor, your humble servant. May I ask a favor of you?

SGANARELLE: What can I do for you, Monsieur Gorgibus?

GORGIBUS: I just happened to meet your brother, who is quite distressed——

SGANARELLE: He's a rascal, Monsieur Gorgibus.

GORGIBUS: But he truly regrets that he made you so angry, and——

SGANARELLE: He's a drunkard, Monsieur Gorgibus.

GORGIBUS: But surely, Doctor, you're not going to give the poor boy up?

SGANARELLE: Not another word about him. The impudence of the rogue, seeking you out to intercede for him! I implore you not to mention him to me.

GORGIBUS: In God's name, Doctor, and out of respect for me, too, have pity on him. I'll do anything for you in return. I promised——

SGANARELLE: You plead so insistently that, even though I swore a violent oath never to forgive him—well, I'll shake your hand on it; I forgive him. You can be assured that I am doing myself a great injury and that I would not have consented to this for any other man. Good-bye, Monsieur Gorgibus.

GORGIBUS: Thank you, Doctor, thank you. I'll go off and look for the boy to tell him the glad news.

> [*He walks off.* SGANARELLE *takes off the doctor's cloak and hat.*]

> [VALÈRE *appears.*]

VALÈRE: I never thought Sganarelle would do his duty so magnificently. Ah, my dear boy, I don't know how to repay you. I'm so happy I——

SGANARELLE: It's easy for you to talk. Gorgibus just ran into me without my doctor's outfit, and if I hadn't come up with a quick story we'd have been sunk. Here he comes again. Disappear.

> [VALÈRE *runs away.*]

> [GORGIBUS *returns.*]

GORGIBUS: Narcissus, I've been looking everywhere for you. I spoke to your brother and he forgives you. But to be safe, I want to see the two of you patch up your quarrel in front of me. Wait here in my house, and I'll find him.

SGANARELLE: I don't think you'll find him, Monsieur. Anyhow, I wouldn't dare to wait; I'm terrified of him.

GORGIBUS: [*pushing* SGANARELLE *inside*] Yes, you will stay. I'm locking you in. Don't be afraid of your brother. I promise you that he's not angry now.

> [*He slams the door and locks it, then goes off to look for the doctor.*]

SGANARELLE: [*at the upstairs window*] Serves me right; I trapped myself and there's no way out. The weather in my future looks threatening, and if there's a storm I'm afraid I'll feel a rain of blows on my back. Or else they'll brand me across the shoulders with a whip—not exactly the brand of medicine any doctor ever prescribed. Yes, I'm in trouble. But why give up when we've come this far? Let's go the limit. I can still make a bid for freedom and prove that Sganarelle is the king of swindlers.

> [*He holds his nose, closes his eyes, and jumps to the ground, just as* GROS-RENÉ *comes back. Then he darts away, picking up the cloak and hat.* GROS-RENÉ *stands staring.*]

GROS-RENÉ: A flying man! What a laugh! I'll wait around and see if there's another one.

> [GORGIBUS *reenters with* SGANARELLE *following him in the doctor's outfit.*]

GORGIBUS: Can't find that doctor. Where the devil has he hidden himself?

> [*He turns and* SGANARELLE *walks into him.*]

There you are. Now, Doctor, I know you said you forgive your brother, but that's not enough. I won't be satisfied until I see you embrace him. He's waiting here in my house.

SGANARELLE: You are joking, Monsieur Gorgibus. Have I not extended myself enough already? I wish never to see him again.

GORGIBUS: Please, Doctor, for me.

SGANARELLE: I cannot refuse when you ask me like that. Tell him to come down.

> [*As* GORGIBUS *goes into the house,* SGANARELLE *drops the clothes, clambers swiftly up to the window again, and scrambles inside.*]

GORGIBUS: [*at the window*] Your brother is waiting for you downstairs, Narcissus. He said he'd do what I asked.

SGANARELLE: [*at the window*] Couldn't you please make him come up here? I beg of you—let me see him in private to ask his forgiveness, because if I go down there he'll show me up and say nasty things to me in front of everybody.

GORGIBUS: All right. Let me tell him.

> [*He leaves the window, and* SGANARELLE *leaps out, swiftly puts on his outfit again, and stands waiting for* GORGIBUS *outside the door.*]

Doctor, he's so ashamed of himself he wants to beg your forgiveness in private, upstairs. Here's the key. Please don't refuse me.

SGANARELLE: There is nothing I would not do for you, Monsieur Gorgibus. You will hear how I deal with him.

> [*He walks into the house and soon appears at the window.* GORGIBUS *has his ear cocked at the door below.* SGANARELLE *alternates his voice, playing the characters one at a time.*]

SGANARELLE: So there you are, you scoundrel!
— Brother, listen to me, please. I'm sorry I knocked those containers over——
— You clumsy ox!
— It wasn't my fault, I swear it.
— Not your fault, you bumpkin? I'll teach you to destroy my work.
— Brother, no, please——
— I'll teach you to trade on Monsieur Gorgibus' good nature. How dare you ask him to ask me to forgive you!
— Brother, I'm sorry, but——
— Silence, you dog!
— I never wanted to hurt you or——
— Silence, I say—

GROS-RENÉ: What exactly do you think is going on up there?

GORGIBUS: It's the doctor and his brother, Narcissus. They had a little disagreement, but now they're making it up.

GROS-RENÉ: Doctor and his brother? But there's only one man.

SGANARELLE: [*at the window*] Yes, you drunkard, I'll thump some good behavior into you. [*pretends to strike a blow*] Ah, he's lowering his eyes; he knows what he's done wrong, the jailbird. And now this hypocrite wants to play the good apostle—

GROS-RENÉ: Just for fun, tell him to let his brother appear at the window.

GORGIBUS: I will. [*to* SGANARELLE] Doctor, let me see your brother for a moment.

SGANARELLE: He is not fit to be seen by an honest gentleman like yourself. Besides, I cannot bear to have him next to me.

GORGIBUS: Please don't say no, after all you've done for me.

SGANARELLE: Monsieur Gorgibus, you have such power over me that I must grant whatever you wish. Show yourself, beast!

> [*He appears at the window as Narcissus.*]

Monsieur Gorgibus, I thank you for your kindness.

> [*He reappears as the doctor.*]

Well, Monsieur, did you take a good look at that image of impurity?

GROS-RENÉ: There's only one man there, Monsieur. We can prove it. Tell them to stand by the window together.

GORGIBUS: Doctor, I want to see you at the window embracing your brother, and then I'll be satisfied.

SGANARELLE: To any other man in the world I would return a swift and negative answer, but to you, Monsieur Gorgibus, I will yield, although not without much pain to myself. But first I want this knave to beg your pardon for all the trouble he has caused you.

> [*He comes back as Narcissus.*]

Yes, Monsieur Gorgibus, I beg your pardon for having bothered you, and I promise you, brother, in front of Monsieur Gorgibus there, that I'll be so good from now on that you'll never be angry with me again. Please let bygones be bygones.

> [*He embraces the cloak and hat.*]

GORGIBUS: There they are, the two of them together.

GROS-RENÉ: The man's a magician.

> [*He hides;* SGANARELLE *comes out of the house, dressed as the doctor.*]

SGANARELLE: Here is your key, Monsieur. I have left my brother inside because I am ashamed of him. One does not wish to be seen in his company now that one has some reputation in this town. You may release him whenever you think fit. Good-bye, Monsieur.

> [*He strides off, then as* GORGIBUS *goes into the house he wheels, dropping the cloak and hat, and climbs back through the window.*]

GORGIBUS: [*upstairs*] There you are, my boy, you're free. I am pleased that your brother forgave you, although I think he was rather hard on you.

SGANARELLE: Monsieur, I cannot thank you enough. A brother's blessing on you. I will remember you all my life.

> [*While they are upstairs,* GROS-RENÉ *has picked up the cloak and hat, and stands waiting for them. They come out of the door.*]

GROS-RENÉ: Well, where do you think your doctor is now?

GORGIBUS: Gone, of course.

GROS-RENÉ: He's right here, under my arm. And by the way, while this fellow was getting in and out of the cloak, the hat, and the window, Valère ran off with your daughter and married her.

GORGIBUS: I'm ruined! I'll have you strung up, you dog, you knave! Yes, you deserve every name your brother called you— What am I saying?

SGANARELLE: You don't really want to string me up, do you, Monsieur? Please listen for one second. It's true that I was having a game with you while my master was with Mademoiselle Lucile. But in serving him I haven't done you any harm. He's a most suitable partner for her, by rank and by income, by God. Believe me, if you make a row about this you'll only bring more confusion on your head. As for that porker there, let him get lost and take Villebrequin with him. Here come our loving couple.

> [VALÈRE *enters contritely with* LUCILE. *They kneel to* GORGIBUS.]

VALÈRE: We apologize to you.

GORGIBUS: Well, perhaps it's lucky that I was tricked by Sganarelle; he's brought me a fine son-in-law. Let's go out to celebrate the marriage and drink a toast to the health of all the company.

[*They dance off in couples:* VALÈRE *with* LUCILE, GORGIBUS *with* GROS-RENÉ, *and* SGANARELLE *with* SABINE.]

CURTAIN

Two Precious Maidens
Ridiculed

Les Précieuses ridicules was billed as a farce for its first production in 1659; most French editions of the play now label it a comedy, as though comedy were inherently superior or more respectable. The play is, of course, farce and comedy at once, swinging from broad and nonsensical moments to tempered irony. It is the ancestor of the satirical comedy of manners, too, although Paul Bénichou shows in his book *La Morale du Grand Siècle* that Molière was on friendly terms with some of the original *précieuses* and would not have wanted to satirize them, but rather the effusions of their successors, who met to celebrate and discuss romantic novels, to talk as though they were characters in those stories, and to swap gossip. The play may owe some inspiration to the Abbé de Pure's novel and play, both entitled *La Précieuse* (1656), and replete with their own euphuisms, and also to Chappuzeau's *The Women's Circle,* which had likewise appeared in 1656. In that same year Saint-Evremond had lightly attacked the affected ladies and their consorts. But it has been claimed that Molière had written a play very like this one before 1655 and that he revised it when he got to Paris. At any rate, nothing as scathing and at the same time amusing had come to public notice before, and it was an instant, roaring success. The *grande dame de la préciosité* Mme de Rambouillet evidently felt that its arrows were not aimed at her, for she invited Molière to mount three performances in her home. And he accepted. He himself played the part of Mascarille in a lugubrious mask—the name means small mask. Jodelet wore the white makeup, mostly flour, for which he was famous. La Grange and Du Croisy played under their own names, following a precedent honored by many actors of the time.

TWO PRECIOUS MAIDENS RIDICULED

Les Précieuses ridicules

CHARACTERS:

LA GRANGE
DU CROISY } rebuffed wooers
GORGIBUS, a respectable, middle-class citizen
MAGDELON, his daughter, a precious maiden
CATHOS, his niece, another precious maiden
MAROTTE, the maidens' maidservant
ALMANZOR, their lackey
Marquis de MASCARILLE, valet to La Grange
Vicomte de JODELET, valet to Du Croisy
Two SEDAN PORTERS
LUCILE and other NEIGHBORS
VIOLINISTS

Scene: [*A drawing room in the house of* GORGIBUS *who has recently moved from a provincial town to Paris*].

[DU CROISY *and* LA GRANGE *are onstage.*]

DU CROISY: La Grange—

LA GRANGE: Yes?

DU CROISY: Listen for a moment and don't laugh.

LA GRANGE: What is it?

DU CROISY: Are you satisfied with our reception here?

LA GRANGE: Have I any reason to be satisfied? Have you?

DU CROISY: Not that I can think of.

LA GRANGE: If you want the truth, I am shocked. Did you ever see two callow girls from the provinces giving themselves such airs? Or two men of the world like us treated with more contempt? They could hardly bring themselves to offer us chairs. I have never seen so many whispers passing between little lips and big ears, so much yawning and rubbing of eyes and asking over and over: "How—aah—late is it?" Whatever we said, did they once answer more than yes or no? Could they have behaved worse if we had been the two least eligible men on earth?

DU CROISY: You are taking the whole thing too seriously.

LA GRANGE: I am indeed, seriously enough to intend to pay them back for their insulting behavior. I know what has made them snub us. It's this precious manner, which first infected Paris and has now spread through the country. These ridiculous hussies have caught a bad attack of it. What an unappetizing mixture: preciousness and flirting! I think I've guessed how a man must behave in order to be welcomed in this house, and if you do your part, we'll put on a little performance that will confront them with their own stupidity and teach them how to appreciate a true gentleman.

DU CROISY: How?

LA GRANGE: My valet, Mascarille, passes himself off among some people as a man of wit and fine manners—nothing is easier to imitate today than fine manners. He plays the fop and sees himself as a man of breeding. He strains to be elegant and to write verse. He turns up his nose at other valets and calls them unrefined.

DU CROISY: What are you going to do about it?

LA GRANGE: I'll tell you, but first let's get away from this house.

[GORGIBUS *comes in.*]

GORGIBUS: Well, gentlemen, you've seen my niece and my daughter. Is everything going well? What are the results of your visit?

LA GRANGE: You had better ask them, rather than us. All we can say is that we are grateful for your kindness, and we remain your humble servants.

[*He bows and goes out with* DU CROISY.]

GORGIBUS: They didn't look very happy. I wonder why. I must ask what happened. Marotte!

[MAROTTE *enters.*]

MAROTTE: Yes, Monsieur?

GORGIBUS: Where are the young ladies?

MAROTTE: In their boudoir.

GORGIBUS: Doing what?

MAROTTE: Making pomade for their lips.

GORGIBUS: I'll pomade them. Tell them to come down. *Start*

[MAROTTE *goes out.*]

Those jades with their pomades are trying to ruin me. I see nothing in this house but whites of eggs, "virgin's milk," and a thousand other mysterious concoctions. Since we've been here they've used up the lard from at least a dozen pigs, and four servants could live out the rest of their days on the sheep's feet they've ground up for their pastes. *↑ depressing*

[MAGDELON *and* CATHOS *enter.*]

Must you spend so much money to grease up your grinning faces? How did you behave toward those gentlemen, to make them leave so coldly? Didn't I order you to welcome them as future husbands?

MAGDELON: But, Father, what about their abominable manner toward us?

CATHOS: Uncle, how can a reasonable girl tolerate men like those?

GORGIBUS: What didn't you like about them?

MAGDELON: A fine sense of chivalry they have—to begin a relationship by treating us like wives!

GORGIBUS: How else would you have them begin? By treating you like concubines? I think they conducted themselves very well, and so should you. The sacred tie of marriage—that's what they are looking forward to. Doesn't it prove that their intentions are sincere?

MAGDELON: Father, you are impossibly bourgeois. I feel ashamed to hear you speaking so bluntly. You ought to learn a little gentility.

GORGIBUS: I don't believe in your hoity-toity talk. I'm a simple man and I tell you that marriage is a simple and holy thing, and if you're honest, you'll talk about it right from the beginning.

MAGDELON: Good Gothic, if everybody thought that, a novel would end as soon as it started. What if Cyrus married Mandane in Chapter One[1] or Aronce were wedded to Clélie[2] without any obstacles instead of having to wait until the end of Volume Ten?

GORGIBUS: What has all this to-do got to do with me?

MAGDELON: Cousin Cathos will tell you the same thing, Father; marriage can take place only after all the other adventures. To make himself acceptable, a lover must know how to utter beautiful thoughts, to pour out tenderness, sweetness, and passion, and —very important—his wooing must follow the rules. First, he meets the maiden he loves in church or out walking or at a public ceremony; or he must be led by Fate—in other words, a friend or relative—to her home, from which he emerges in a dream or state of melancholy. For a time he hides his devotion from his beloved, but he does pay her several visits and joins in discussions of gallantry; this never fails to edify the assembled guests. The day comes for his declaration and this is usually made along some garden path, when the rest of the company has moved out of range. The message of love promptly enrages us—our blushes indicate this clearly—and the young man is thereby banished from our presence, for a short time. He next finds some way of appeasing us; gradually we soften to his passionate recital, and he draws out our own vows, which are unbearably painful to confess. After that come the adventures: the rivals who throw themselves in the way of true love; the persecutions of the fathers; the jealousy caused by misunderstanding; the accusations, the heartaches, the abductions, and other assorted complications. That's how these affairs unwind; there are rules of chivalry and breeding that must be observed. But to leap from one end of the love affair to the other, to substitute a marriage contract for an amour, to seize the novel by its tail—nothing, Father, nothing could be more commercial, and the mere thought of it makes my heart shiver.

---

[1] Of Mlle de Scudéry's *Grand Cyrus*, a popular "precious" novel of the seventeenth century.

[2] The hero and heroine of *Clélie*, another formidably long novel by Mlle de Scudéry, one of "those voluminous works commonly called Romances, namely, *Clelia, Cleopatra, Astraea, Cassandra, The Grand Cyrus*, and innumerable others which contain, as I apprehend, very little instruction or entertainment . . ."—Henry Fielding, in his preface to *Joseph Andrews*.

GORGIBUS: What the devil is all this jargon? Is that what they call high style?

CATHOS: Cousin Magdelon has described it exquisitely, Uncle. How can we welcome men who have only the crudest idea of gallantry? I'd wager that they have never seen the Map of the Lovescape; they are quite unfamiliar with such place-names as Love-letters, Tiny-attentions, Gallant-words, and Pretty-poems.[3] Their very appearance lacks that gracious air that impresses people. Coming to court us without a ribbon on their calves or a plume in their hats! Without touching up their hair after they walk in! And wearing clothes with not a single decoration on them! Good high heaven, what sort of lovers are they! With their drab outfits and dreary conversation, we couldn't possibly have gone any farther with them. Their shirtfronts come from the wrong tailor and their breeches are six noticeable inches too narrow.

GORGIBUS: They're off their rockers, both of them. I can't understand a word of this gibberish, Cathos, and you, Magdelon——

MAGDELON: Please, Father, don't address us by those outlandish names. Call us something more suitable.

GORGIBUS: Outlandish names! Aren't they the names you were baptized with?

MAGDELON: You are simply common. I am astonished that a man like you could have had a daughter of my quality. Can you imagine any novelist calling her characters Cathos or Magdelon? Either of those names would be enough to deface the finest story ever written.

CATHOS: That is true, Uncle; a delicate ear suffers on hearing words like those. The names my cousin and I have chosen for ourselves, Polyxene and Aminte,[4] are far more graceful, you must agree.

GORGIBUS: Listen to me. I don't see why you should have any names other than the ones given you by your godfathers and godmothers. As for those gentlemen we were talking about, I know their

---

[3] *La Carte de Tendre,* literally the Map of Tenderness, was another invention of Mlle de Scudéry; lovers were supposed to progress through such allegorical cities and landmarks as "Newborn-friendship" and "Great-wit." The map appears in the novel *Clélie.*

[4] More names suggested by the example of Mlle de Scudéry, who referred to herself as Sappho, and by Mme de Rambouillet, whom her followers reverently called Arthénice.

families and properties, and I've made up my mind that you are going to welcome them as your husbands. I'm fed up with having you on my hands. Keeping two girls out of mischief is too much trouble for a man of my age.

CATHOS: All I can say to you, Uncle, is that I consider marriage quite distasteful. How can one support the thought of lying beside a man who is literally naked?

MAGDELON: We have only just arrived here. Let us breathe awhile in Paris society and create the novel of our lives at leisure; don't rush us into the ending.

GORGIBUS: [*aside*] No doubt about it; they're over the edge. [*aloud*] I can't follow any of this twaddle. I am the master of this house. That's the end of the discussion. Either you get married, both of you—and soon—or I'll make nuns of you. I take my oath on it.

[*He goes out.*]

CATHOS: Your father's form, dear, is so buried in content. His intelligence is mud and there is darkness in his soul.

MAGDELON: He embarrasses me. I cannot persuade myself that I am his daughter. One day, I think, some adventure will reveal that my birth was in truth illustrious.

CATHOS: Everything points to it. And personally, when I look at myself——

[MAROTTE *enters.*]

MAROTTE: There's a man here who wants to know if you're at home. Says his master would like to see you.

MAGDELON: Oh, you idiot. Learn to announce yourself with less vulgarity. Say: "A necessary nuisance requests whether you are in a convenient state to be attended upon."

MAROTTE: Me, I don't understand Latin, and I haven't picked up my filofosy from those novels you read.

MAGDELON: Impertinent creature, how do I ever put up with you! Well, who is the master of this necessary nuisance?

MAROTTE: Says he's called the Marquess de Mascarille.

MAGDELON: [*to* CATHOS] My dear, a marquess! [*to* MAROTTE] Good, go and say that he may make his entrance. [*to* CATHOS] He must be a society wit who has already heard of us.

CATHOS: Oh, definitely.

MAGDELON: We will have to receive him down here, rather than in the boudoir. Let's tidy our hair and make good on our reputation. [*to* MAROTTE] Quickly, repair to the inner chamber with our silver beauty counselor.

MAROTTE: Lord slap me down if I know what you're on about. You'll have to stop talking heathen if you want me to follow.

MAGDELON: Fetch us the mirror, fool, and make sure you don't soil the glass by reflecting your image in it.

[MAROTTE, MAGDELON, *and* CATHOS *hurry out.*]

[MASCARILLE *enters in a sedan chair, carried by two* PORTERS.]

MASCARILLE: Stop, porters, stop. There, there, there, there, there! I think these rogues mean to destroy me by banging this sedan against every wall and flagstone.

FIRST PORTER: Hell, it's a narrow doorway. You wanted us to bring you all the way in.

MASCARILLE: Certainly I did. Rascals, do you want me to expose the extremities of my plumes to the unkindness of the damp season? And to imprint my footwear in mud? Begone, and take your sedan with you.

SECOND PORTER: Are you going to pay us, please, Monsieur?

MASCARILLE: What was that?

SECOND PORTER: I asked if you'd be so good as to pay us.

MASCARILLE: [*clouting him*] What, you knave, asking a person of my quality for money!

SECOND PORTER: This is how poor people get paid. Is your quality going to give us our dinner?

MASCARILLE: I'll soon teach you who you are. Do these rabble dare to trifle with me?

FIRST PORTER: [*removing one of the sedan pole handles*] Now pay us, quick!

MASCARILLE: Eh?

FIRST PORTER: I said I want my money—now!

MASCARILLE: This man is reasonable.

FIRST PORTER: Hurry up.

MASCARILLE: Yes, yes. I like the way you ask. But this one is a knave; he doesn't know how to ask. There; are you satisfied?

FIRST PORTER: No, I'm not satisfied. You clouted my pal's face.

MASCARILLE: Don't be offended. Here, this will pay for the blow. You can have anything of me as long as you ask decently. Away you go, and come back later to take me to the Louvre, into the King's inner sanctum.

[*The* PORTERS *go out, with their sedan.*]

[MAROTTE *comes in.*]

MAROTTE: Monsieur, the ladies will be here in a minute.

MASCARILLE: Tell them not to hurry. I am comfortably installed to await them.

MAROTTE: Here they are.

[MAROTTE *goes out.*]

[MAGDELON *and* CATHOS *enter with* ALMANZOR.]

MASCARILLE: Dear ladies, you will be surprised, no doubt, at the audacity of my visit; but your reputation has wished this tiresome encounter on you, and your excellence exerts so powerful a charm on me that I would race everywhere to pursue it.

MAGDELON: Oh, Monsieur, it is not on our lands that you should hunt for excellence.

CATHOS: If there be excellence here, it is you who have brought it.

MASCARILLE: Ah, no, ladies. I register a protest against your words. Renown has indeed paid you fair tribute, and you will win every game in the elegant world of Paris, *pic, repic,* and *capot,* as we say in picquet.[5]

MAGDELON: Your tongue, Monsieur, is too liberal with its praise. My cousin and I will endeavor not to take its sweet flattery too much to heart.

CATHOS: My dear, we have need of chairs.

MAGDELON: Almanzor, hither!

---

[5] A fashionable French card game. *Pic, repic,* and *capot* means an outright and immediate victory. The sentence may be read more simply as: "You will win hands down in the elegant world of Paris."

ALMANZOR: Madame?

MAGDELON: Quickly, array the commodities of conversation.

[ALMANZOR *goes out.*]

MASCARILLE: But am I safe here?

CATHOS: Why, what do you fear?

MASCARILLE: The theft of my heart and the assassination of my liberty. I see eyes about me that are like naughty boys, ready to capture me and treat me like a Moorish prisoner of the Turks. No sooner do I approach them than they stand murderously on guard. By my soul, I do not trust them; I must flee, unless you promise they shall do me no harm.

MAGDELON: My dear, he is The Lively Character to the life.

CATHOS: A true Hamilcar.[6]

MAGDELON: Do not be afraid. Our eyes have no wicked designs on you and your heart may rest assured of their probity.

CATHOS: But please, Monsieur, do not resist this chair, which has been holding out its arms. Satisfy its desire to embrace you.

[MASCARILLE *looks into a pocket mirror as he combs and pats his hair. He then adjusts the waist of his breeches.*]

MASCARILLE: Well, ladies, what do you say to Paris?

MAGDELON: What can we say? It would be the obverse of reason to deny that Paris is the great office of marvels, the center of good taste, high wit, and chivalry.

MASCARILLE: For myself, I hold that beyond Paris there is no healthy life for decent people.

CATHOS: An unmitigable truth.

MASCARILLE: It does grow rather muddy, but one has one's sedan.

MAGDELON: One does indeed. The sedan is a miraculous stronghold against the onslaughts of mud and ill weather.

MASCARILLE: Do you receive many visitors? Who is your leading personality?

MAGDELON: Unhappily, we are not yet known. But we are becoming acquainted and we are now close to a lady who has promised to

---

[6] A character described as "lively" in the novel *Clélie.*

bring us all the gentlemen who contributed to the anthologies in *The Sheaf of Collected Fragments.*[7]

CATHOS: As well as certain other gentlemen who have been recommended to us as sovereign arbiters of good taste.

MASCARILLE: I can attend to this better than anybody; they all come to visit me, and I can honestly say that I never get out of bed without finding a half-dozen great minds waiting to pay court to me.

MAGDELON: We would be beholden to you, Monsieur, to the deepest depth, if you could do us this kindness; for after all we must meet all those gentlemen if we are to belong to the cream of society. They are the men who confer reputations in Paris; and as you know, a single visit from any of them is enough to establish a person as being in the know; nothing else is necessary. These brilliant gatherings teach you hundreds of things you simply must be aware of: the essence of sophistication. As you become acquainted with them you learn new witticisms from the pretty exchanges of prose and verse. You hear about it as soon as So-and-so writes the most delightful little item in the world on such and such a topic; a certain lady has married words to a bare melody; this one has composed a madrigal to celebrate a conquest; that one has thrown off a few stanzas to bewail an infidelity; Monsieur X last night wrote a six-line poem to Mademoiselle Y, to which she sent a reply at eight o'clock this morning; Author A has just finished the outline of his new novel; Author B is well advanced into the third part of his; Author C is just sending his to the printer. This is the sort of thing that makes you respected, and if you cannot keep up with it, I would not give a brass tack for all your wit.

CATHOS: Yes, I find it utterly ridiculous for a person to think he can keep up with the world unless he knows about the tiniest four-line verse that is written that day. Why, I would die of shame if someone asked me if I had seen a new poem and I hadn't.

MASCARILLE: True, it is downright embarrassing not to be a party to everything the moment it is written. But don't be disturbed. I will establish a French Academy of Fine Minds here, in your home,

[7] Probably a reference to a volume published in 1658 by the Bercy Bookstore under the title "Selected short works of Corneille, Bensérade, de Scudéry, Sarrazin, etc."

and I guarantee that there will not be one smattering of poetry in Paris that you won't know by heart before anyone else. I may say in all modesty that I scribble myself when I feel like it, and as they flow through the most exclusive channels in Paris, you are likely to hear some two hundred of my songs, an equal number of sonnets, four hundred epigrams, and more than a thousand madrigals, without counting my enigmas and profiles.

MAGDELON: I am furiously fond of profiles; I think that nothing flashes with the dazzle of a profile.

MASCARILLE: Profiles are difficult; they call for a profound mind. You will see a few of mine that may not displease you.

CATHOS: I, as it happens, am devoted to enigmas.

MASCARILLE: Now *they* put the intelligence through its paces. I tossed off four this morning. I'll give them to you to work out.

MAGDELON: Madrigals are enchanting when they are well formed.

MASCARILLE: My special talent! I am composing a history, in madrigals, of the Roman Empire.

MAGDELON: That will be the most bewitching thing. I must claim a copy, if you have it published.

MASCARILLE: You shall each have a copy, I promise, in the finest binding. It is, of course, below my dignity and standing to publish books in my own name. I allow them in print only so that all the booksellers who keep plaguing me can earn some money.

MAGDELON: It must give you great pleasure to see yourself on the printed page.

MASCARILLE: I suppose so. That reminds me; I absolutely must recite an impromptu. I wrote it yesterday during a visit to a friend—a duchess, you know. I'm devilishly powerful when it comes to impromptus.

CATHOS: The impromptu is the ultimate touchstone of wit.

MASCARILLE: Listen to this one.

MAGDELON: We are all ears.

MASCARILLE:

> Oh, oh, I could not have been on guard,
> For when I innocently stared at you too hard,
> Your sly little eye stole my heart. O grief!
> Stop thief, stop thief, stop thief, stop thief!

CATHOS: Heavenly. Expressed with the utmost delicacy.

MASCARILLE: Everything I do has that spontaneous touch. It never reeks of the pedant, or even the scholar.

MAGDELON: It's the other end of the universe.

MASCARILLE: Did you notice the opening: *Oh, oh?* Something extraordinary has happened, and so—*Oh, oh!* Like a man who becomes aware, all of a sudden—*Oh, oh!* A surprise—*Oh, oh!*

MAGDELON: It's such an expressive *Oh, oh.*

MASCARILLE: It doesn't seem like much.

CATHOS: What are you saying? It is one of those statements that are priceless.

MAGDELON: Nothing less. I would rather have written that *Oh, oh* than an epic poem.

MASCARILLE: 'Sblood, but you have good taste.

MAGDELON: Quite good.

MASCARILLE: But don't you like that *I could not have been on guard,* too? *I could not have been on guard,* meaning: I was not watching out when I should have been, but a more natural way of saying it: *I could not have been on guard.* Next—*For when I innocently:* that is, without malice or wrong intention, like a poor sheep. *Stared at you too hard:* in other words, I considered you, I observed you, I contemplated you. *Your sly little eye*—what do you think of that word *sly?* Plucked from a field of alternatives. Isn't it well chosen?

CATHOS: Methodically.

MASCARILLE: *Sly:* cunning, furtive, like a cat who has just caught a mouse. *Sly.*

MAGDELON: It could not be more apt.

MASCARILLE: *Stole my heart:* carried it away, robbed me of it. *Stop thief, stop thief, stop thief, stop thief!* Wouldn't you say that's a man shouting and running after a thief to make him stop? *Stop thief, stop thief, stop thief, stop thief!*

MAGDELON: It has a menacing and mysterious ring.

MASCARILLE: Would you like to hear the melody I put to it?

CATHOS: Oh, you've studied music?

MASCARILLE: I? Never.

CATHOS: Then how did you compose it?

MASCARILLE: Men of quality know everything without having to learn anything.

MAGDELON: Of course, dear.

MASCARILLE: Tell me if you like the melody. [*clears his throat*] La, la, la, la, la—mi, mi, mi—sol, do. Brutal weather always mutilates my voice. But it doesn't matter; this is only an amateur performance. [*singing*]

> Oh, oh, I could not have been on guard.
> For when I innocently stared at you too hard,
> Your sly little eye stole my heart. O grief!
> Stop thief, stop thief, stop thief, stop thief!

CATHOS: What passion there is in that melody. I could die of it!

MAGDELON: Positively crammed with chromatics.

MASCARILLE: Don't you agree that the music finds its expression in the thought, and vice versa? *Stop thief!* And then, as if the cry were growing louder: *stop, stop, stop, stop, stop, stop, thief!*

MAGDELON: It's the last thing of all, but the very last, the great last, the last of the last. It is a marvel! I am captured—by the melody *and* the words.

CATHOS: I have never been exposed to anything so forceful.

MASCARILLE: Whatever I do comes to me naturally, without study.

MAGDELON: Nature has treated you like an indulgent mother; and you are her spoiled child.

MASCARILLE: Tell me, how do you spend your days?

CATHOS: Doing nothing.

MAGDELON: Until now we have been starved of entertainment.

MASCARILLE: Would you like me to escort you to the theater one day soon? They should be performing a little something that I would like us to see together.

MAGDELON: How could we refuse?

MASCARILLE: But I must ask you to applaud in the right places. I am committed to the play's success; the author came to see me about it this morning. We have a custom in Paris: authors come to us men of quality to read us their new plays, and if possible, to win our approval in advance, so as to secure their reputations. As you can imagine, once we have read something and liked it, nobody in the cheap seats dares to contradict us. I am a man of scruple, and when I give a playwright my promise I always shout, "Author, author!" before the houselights go up.

MAGDELON: We understand perfectly. Paris is a scintillating place and a hundred things happen every day that we know nothing about in the provinces, however brilliant we may be.

CATHOS: You have told us enough. Now that we know we will do our duty and shriek our admiration—in the right places—at every word that is spoken.

MASCARILLE: [*to* MAGDELON] I may be wrong, but you seem to me like somebody who has written a play.

MAGDELON: I don't deny that there may be something in what you say.

MASCARILLE: We must see it. Between ourselves, I have completed one that I intend to have staged.

CATHOS: What company will you give it to?

MASCARILLE: What a question! Naturally, to the Bourgogne Players.[8] They are the only ones who know how to play for effect. The others are ignorant fellows who talk like people. They don't know how to snort out their lines or pause at a strategic point. And how can we recognize a fine line if the actor doesn't pause to warn us that it is time to show our appreciation?

CATHOS: That is the only way to let the audience *feel* the beauty of a work. Lines are worth no more than the actors endow them with.

MASCARILLE: By the by, what do you think of my accouterments? Don't you find them suited to this outfit?

CATHOS: Ineffably.

MASCARILLE: The ribbon is well matched, isn't it?

MAGDELON: Furiously well. It's pure Paris.[9]

MASCARILLE: What do you say to my garters?

MAGDELON: They look terribly right.

MASCARILLE: Without boasting, I must mention that they are a comfortable twelve inches wider than the ready-made variety.

[8] *Les Grands Comédiens* of the Hotel de Bourgogne were Molière's competitors.
[9] Literally, "pure Perdrigeon," the name of a fashionable merchant.

MAGDELON: I have never *seen* such prepossessing accessories.

MASCARILLE: Bring your nasal passages within perfume range of these gloves.

MAGDELON: They smell fanatically good.

CATHOS: I have never breathed a more elusive fragrance.

MASCARILLE: Now inhale my wig.

MAGDELON: Oh, how subtle! It touches the brain deliciously.

MASCARILLE: You haven't told me about my plumes. What do you think?

CATHOS: Paralyzingly beautiful.

MASCARILLE: Can you believe that the headpiece cost me a whole gold coin? I have a mania: I veer only toward what is finest.

MAGDELON: You and I are one: rigidly particular about clothing. Right down to my understockings I cannot bear anything that doesn't come from the most expensive seamstress.

MASCARILLE: [*crying out suddenly*] Ah, gently, gently! Damn my eyes, ladies, but you're being unfair. You're taking advantage of me. It's not honest.

CATHOS: What isn't? What's wrong?

MASCARILLE: Both of you against my heart at the same time, attacking me from the right and the left. It's against the rules of warfare; the struggle is unequal; I must cry "Murder."

CATHOS: He has such an individual way of saying things.

MAGDELON: He has an inimitable turn of phrase.

CATHOS: You are more afraid than injured. Your heart cries out before it has been damaged.

MASCARILLE: The devil take me if it isn't damaged—from head to foot.

[MAROTTE *enters.*]

MAROTTE: Madame, somebody to see you.

MAGDELON: [*reading a visiting card*] The Vicomte de Jodelet.

MASCARILLE: Jodelet?

MAROTTE: Yes, Monsieur.

CATHOS: Do you know him?

MASCARILLE: He is my best friend.

MAGDELON: Ask him to come swiftly in.

[MAROTTE *goes out.*]

MASCARILLE: It's some time since we last saw each other. I am over-joyed at this lucky encounter.

CATHOS: Here he is.

[ALMANZOR *enters with* JODELET, *who has a limp.*]

MASCARILLE: *Vicomte!*

[*They kiss each other's cheeks.*]

JODELET: *Marquess!*

MASCARILLE: What a surprise!

JODELET: What a delight!

MASCARILLE: One more little kiss, please.

MAGDELON: [*to* CATHOS] We, my sweet, are becoming known. Society is walking up to our front door.

MASCARILLE: Ladies, allow me to present this gentleman. I swear that he is worth your acquaintance.

JODELET: I come to pay you the homage you deserve. Your charms demand their *droits de seigneur* from any man.

MAGDELON: You are extending your kindness to the farther limits of flattery.

CATHOS: We must mark this date on our calendar as a day of high fortune.

MAGDELON: [*to* ALMANZOR] Come along, boy, must I repeat everything? You can see that we need a supplemental chair.

MASCARILLE: Don't be surprised if the Vicomte's face is rather wan. He has just recovered from a seizure.

JODELET: The fruit of long nights in the palace and the fatigues of warfare.

MASCARILLE: Do you know, ladies, that in the Vicomte you see one of the most valiant men of the century—a paragon of courage!

JODELET: You are no less, Marquess. We know what you too are capable of.

MASCARILLE: It is true that we were together wherever the fighting was thickest.

JODELET: And the heat hottest!

MASCARILLE: Yes, but not as hot as it is here, eh? Ha, ha, ha!

JODELET: We met in the army. The first time we ever saw each other he was commanding a regiment of horse in the Maltese galleys.

MASCARILLE: But you enlisted before I did. I was only a subaltern when you were in charge of 2,000 cavalrymen.

JODELET: Yes. War is a fine thing, but damn my wounds, today there's almost no recognition from Court for distinguished men of arms like us.

MASCARILLE: I am tempted to hang up my sword.

CATHOS: I must say that I have a leaning toward swordsmen.

MAGDELON: I admire them too, but I like my bravery seasoned with wit.

MASCARILLE: Vicomte, do you remember that crescent-shaped fortress we seized from the enemy at the Siege of Arras?

JODELET: What do you mean, crescent-shaped? It was a full moon.

MASCARILLE: I think you must be right.

JODELET: I ought to remember, by God. I was wounded in the leg by a grenade. I still carry the scars. Touch it lightly. You'll feel the lump. That's it.

CATHOS: The scar is enormous.

MASCARILLE: Give me your hand a moment, and feel this, at the back of my head. Have you got it?

MAGDELON: I can certainly feel something.

MASCARILLE: A musket volley that I took full blast during my last campaign.

JODELET: [*baring his chest*] Here's a bullet that went in one side of me and out the other when I was attacking at Gravelines.

MASCARILLE: [*putting his hand on the button of his breeches*] And now I am going to show you a truly wicked wound.

MAGDELON: You need not. We believe you without seeing it.

MASCARILLE: These are marks of honor. They prove what kind of a man I am.

CATHOS: We can see what kind of a man you are.

MASCARILLE: Vicomte, is your coach outside?

JODELET: Why?

MASCARILLE: We could take the ladies for a ride and some **refreshment.**

MAGDELON: But we can't go out today.

MASCARILLE: Then let us have some violins for dancing here.

JODELET: By God, that's an idea.

MAGDELON: We'd love that, but we shall need more company.

MASCARILLE: Where are my servants? Champagne, Picardy, Burgundy, Cascaret, Basque, la Verdure, Lorraine, Provence, la Violette! May they all be damned! I don't think there's another nobleman in France as badly attended as I am. They always desert me, the scum.

MAGDELON: Almanzor, go out and tell the Marquess' men to find some violinists; and invite in a few ladies and gentlemen from the neighborhood, to share our lonely ball.

[ALMANZOR *goes out.*]

MASCARILLE: Vicomte, what do you say to these eyes?

JODELET: I say: what do *you* say?

MASCARILLE: I say that our freedom will have a difficult time leaving this house in one piece. I keep feeling a strange thumping. My heart is hanging by a single thread.

MAGDELON: Everything he says sounds so natural. He contrives the most beautiful language in the world.

CATHOS: Yes, he expends his wit furiously.

MASCARILLE: To show you that I don't exaggerate, I am going to make up an impromptu based on that statement.

CATHOS: Oh, yes, I beg you with all my heart; give us a little something written especially for us.

JODELET: I'd do the same, but at the moment my poetic veins are dry. I have been bled too many times in the last few days.

MASCARILLE: What can be holding me back? The first line always comes easily enough; it's the others that generally give me trouble. I am trying to rush myself; better if I take longer over this impromptu, and when it is finished you will have to admit that it is the most authentic one ever written.

JODELET: He has the verbal verve of a demon.

MAGDELON: And the chivalry; and the style.

MASCARILLE: Vicomte, tell me, is it long since you saw the Comtesse?

JODELET: My last visit was over three weeks ago.

MASCARILLE: Would you believe this? The Duke came to see me this morning and invited me to hunt stag with him in the country.

MAGDELON: Here come our friends.

[LUCILE *enters with other neighbors. Behind them:* MAROTTE *and a group of violinists.*]

MAGDELON: My dear friends, we beg your pardon. These gentlemen had the inspiration of dancing to these sweet-singing catguts, and we sent for you to populate the voids in our company.

LUCILE: We are honored.

MASCARILLE: This is no more than a makeshift dance, but one of these days we shall hold a formal ball. Are the violins ready?

ALMANZOR: Yes, Monsieur, ready.

CATHOS: Then let us take our places, ladies.

MASCARILLE: [*dancing alone, as a prelude*] La, la, la, la, la, la, la, la.

MAGDELON: He has such an *elegant* physique.

CATHOS: And he carries himself like a dancer.

MASCARILLE: [*seizing* MAGDELON] With every step I take I trade my freedom underfoot. Keep the rhythm, vile violins, keep the rhythm. Oh, the ignorami! Impossible to follow their beat. Confound you, don't you know how to play in time? La, la, la, la, la, la, la, la. A firm beat, you rural scrapers.

JODELET: [*also dancing*] Don't push the speed so hard. I've scarcely left my sickbed.

[DU CROISY *and* LA GRANGE *come in.*]

LA GRANGE: Scoundrels, what are you doing here? We've been looking for you for hours.

[*He beats* MASCARILLE.]

MASCARILLE: Ow, ooh, ah, oh. You didn't say I'd get a beating.

[DU CROISY *beats* JODELET.]

JODELET: Wow, ow, ooooh!

LA GRANGE: You deserve this for trying to play the gentleman.

DU CROISY: This will show you who you really are.

[DU CROISY *and* LA GRANGE *go out.*]

MAGDELON: What was that about?

JODELET: A wager.

CATHOS: What? To let yourselves be thrashed like that?

MASCARILLE: Good God, I'm not going to let a little thing like a thrashing annoy me. I'm a violent man. Daren't let myself get carried away.

MAGDELON: How could you put up with such an insult in front of us?

MASCARILLE: It was nothing. I wouldn't even discuss, let alone resent, a trivial matter like a beating-up when it comes from an old friend.

[DU CROISY *and* LA GRANGE *return.*]

LA GRANGE: So you think you can laugh at us behind our backs, do you, hyenas?[10]

MAGDELON: What do you mean by coming into our house and upsetting us like this?

DU CROISY: What do *you* mean, ladies, by welcoming our lackeys more warmly than us? Letting them woo you at our expense? Letting them throw a dance for you?

MAGDELON: Your lackeys?

LA GRANGE: Our lackeys. It's neither fair nor honest of you to distract them from their work.

MAGDELON: Oh, what insolence!

LA GRANGE: But they won't hide inside our clothes any longer. From now on, if you like them it will be for the color of their eyes. [*to* JODELET *and* MASCARILLE] Strip down immediately.

JODELET: [*undressing*] Farewell, my finery!

MASCARILLE: [*undressing*] The Marquess and the Vicomte fall to the floor.

DU CROISY: So you thought you'd trespass on our territory? You'll have to find some better way to impress your beauties.

LA GRANGE: It's too much; to take our places—in our clothes!

MASCARILLE: O fortune, thou art inconstant!

---

[10] At this point, La Grange calls in some "others," presumably servants, to manhandle Mascarille and Jodelet and undress them; but the sequence may be equally—or more—effective without the "others."

DU CROISY: Hurry up. Get those garments off, every one of them.

> [JODELET *is removing a parade of colored underwear.*]

LA GRANGE: Now, take all those clothes away. Hurry! And so, ladies, we leave you to continue your relations with them in this state of nature, for as long as you wish. We grant you full permission to do so and I assure you that this gentleman and I will not be in the least jealous.

> [LA GRANGE *and* DU CROISY *go out.*]

CATHOS: Oh, confusion!

MAGDELON: I am boiling with shame.

FIRST VIOLINIST: What's going on? Who's going to pay us?

MASCARILLE: Ask the Vicomte.

FIRST VIOLINIST: Who'll give us our money?

JODELET: Ask the Marquess.

> [GORGIBUS *comes in.*]

GORGIBUS: Vixens! What are you trying to do—send me to my winding-sheets? I've just heard about this affair from the gentlemen who went out.

MAGDELON: Father, they played a filthy trick on us.

GORGIBUS: It's your own fault. But I'm the poor creature that has to swallow the insult.

MAGDELON: I swear we'll have our revenge on them, or I'll die from the disgrace. [*to* MASCARILLE *and* JODELET] Are you still here, you impostors, after that pretense?

MASCARILLE: A nice way to talk to a marquess! That's how it is in society: the slightest mishap and people who cherish you one moment despise you the next. Come, my friend, we will go and find our fortune elsewhere. It is plain to me that the people in this house worship outward appearance and have no respect for naked virtue.

> [MASCARILLE *and* JODELET *go out in their underwear.*]

FIRST VIOLINIST: Monsieur, they haven't paid for our playing, so we'll have to ask you.

GORGIBUS: [*beating them*] Yes, yes, I'll pay you: here's your salary. [*Exit* VIOLINISTS, *running.*] And I don't know what stops me from doing the same thing to the two of you. We'll be the butt and the laughingstock of everybody; that's what comes of your showing off. Run away and hide from my sight. [*Exit* MAGDELON *and* CATHOS.] And you [*flinging about books and papers from a table*], you're responsible for their madness, you stupid books, you buncombe, you pernicious entertainments for lazy minds, you romances, fancies, songs, verse, and worse—may you all feed the biggest bonfire in hell!

CURTAIN

Sganarelle, or the Imaginary Cuckold

Sganarelle, ou le Cocu imaginaire, a verse comedy, came to be Molière's most frequently produced work during his lifetime, and it has retained some popularity among French audiences, although it has never been translated before into English rhyming verse. It had its first showing in May, 1660, about six months after the premiere of *Les Précieuses ridicules,* and was an even greater success, enjoying thirty-four performances during the summer. One enthusiastic spectator named Neufvillaine kept going to see it until he had memorized it; he then offered it to a printer. But Molière heard about the piracy in time and managed to make a royalty arrangement for the publication. Some of his contemporaries felt that he had taken a step backward in returning to Italian farce for his material, but others praised the play extravagantly for its style, its plotting, its insights, and above all, its characters. One current criticism was that the story leaned on coincidences; the finding of the locket with Lélie's portrait in it leads to suspicions on the part of the principal quartet: Sganarelle, his wife, Célie, and Lélie. Yet this coincidence is made to function brilliantly; the play springs from a single incident and works because all the characters have the suspicions *before* it happens; they are already prepared to believe the worst. The play includes some resounding speeches, notably Sganarelle's discussion of honor, not unlike, in its own way, Falstaff's great speech in *Henry IV, Part I,* which was written at least sixty years earlier but followed a different development. (There is no way of knowing whether Molière was familiar with Shakespeare's play; a careful comparison of the two speeches suggests that the resemblance is a literary accident, although Molière would not have hesitated to draw on Shakespeare's work if he had known and liked it, any more than Shakespeare would have scrupled to borrow from where he saw fit.) The play does not belong exclusively to Sganarelle, although that was the part Molière played—his first without a mask. Célie and Lélie are negligible acts of the imagination; as presences they serve some of the scenes effectively, especially the one in which Sganarelle believes that Célie is sympathizing with him when she is pitying herself; but the lovers' language and ideas are ridden with conventional sighs and doubts. Gorgibus, Martine, and Lisette, however, are colorful types and so, during his brief appearance, is Gros-René, the traditional, ever-famished fat man. The verse is an unusual blending of poetry and the vernacular. Ramón Fernández calls it "homely everyday speech with its sonorities amplified, so that they reverberate in the mind and affect us as song does."

In translating this play I have resorted from time to time to the break halfway along the line. This break is common, almost obligatory, in Racine, Corneille, and Molière, though it is often disguised by an "and" or a "but," and is not always punctuated. I have also tried deliberately to avoid the repetition of Molière's vocabulary. In French verse drama it becomes something of a game to see in how many ways such words as *affront, criminel, reprocher, flammes, coeur, audace, foi,* and *honneur* can be used and with what reaches of meaning. Their English equivalents, however, have less resonance in sound and suggestiveness. One final apologetic explanation: I have used the feminine rhyme with more abandon than in the original, and can only plead a) that the stress in French falls naturally on second syllables and in English does not—in other words, the feminine rhyme is less unnatural in English; b) that the relative poverty of rhymes in English forces a translator to stretch at times for almost impermissible (at least, unorthodox) rhymes, if he does not want to repeat line endings.

SGANARELLE, OR THE IMAGINARY CUCKOLD

Sganarelle, ou le Cocu imaginaire

CHARACTERS:

GORGIBUS, a middle-class citizen
CÉLIE, his daughter
LÉLIE, young man in love with Célie
GROS-RENÉ, his valet
SGANARELLE, another citizen, neighbor of Gorgibus
MARTINE,* his wife
VILLEBREQUIN, father of Valère, Célie's intended
LISETTE,* Célie's chaperone
DORANTE,* Sganarelle's father-in-law
TWO SERVANTS

The scene is Paris.

[*In front of the houses of* GORGIBUS *and* SGANAR-
ELLE, *in a suburb of Paris.* CÉLIE, *looking tearful,
comes out of* GORGIBUS' *house, followed by her father
and* LISETTE, *her chaperone.*]

CÉLIE: No, Father; I will not agree to that.

GORGIBUS: What are you muttering there, you stubborn brat?
           How dare you argue when I've had my say!
           Do I or don't I have unquestioned sway
           Over you? Or are daughters, by your lights,
           Allowed to trample on their fathers' rights?

* These characters have no names in the French, but are known simply
as "Sganarelle's wife," "Célie's chaperone" and "a relative of Sganarelle's
wife." The names are added here to facilitate casting and identification.

71

Which of us makes the law here? Tell me who,
In your opinion, knows what's best for you?
I'd better warn you now: this infantile
Defiance is bound to stimulate my bile,
And if you drive me to my last resource
You'll soon feel whether my arm has lost its force.
In other words, Miss Mutineer, be wise,
Forget this nonsense, and accept the prize
I'm offering you. You think I've no idea
What sort of man comes with it? Have no fear.
I'm told Valère is well provided for—
A private fortune—who could ask for more?
These twenty thousand ducats he'll inherit
Are yours for love, provided you can spare it.
Who cares about his faults when every taint
Is worth its weight in gold? The boy's a saint.

CÉLIE: Alas—

GORGIBUS: Alas? What's that supposed to mean?
I hate alases. Don't you make a scene,
My girl, and rouse my blood, or very soon
You'll sing *alas* to quite a different tune.
No wonder you're obsessed by stupid fancies
When day and night you read these cheap romances,
Which fill your head with love, instead of higher
And holier matter—fling them in the fire
Before they wreck your morals, as in truth
They've undermined so many of our youth.
Get hold of books that deal with good behavior
By stressing the examples of our Saviour
And of our statesmen: thoughtful books of saws,
Precepts, and proverbs, common sense and laws.
Learn them by heart. The best of all's the one
Called *Sinners*, written by a Spanish nun.
They'll teach you how to live and to correct
Your failings and to pick up some respect
For me.

CÉLIE: But, Father, how can I forget
That I'm engaged to Lélie? If I let
You talk me into this, I still defy
Your orders; you selected him, not I.

GORGIBUS: Lélie's a pleasant fellow, but who needs him
When someone comes along who supersedes him?
I simply fail to see how he competes
With all that wealth; his looks are mere conceits.
But good old gold has its peculiar charms;
It flattens opposition and disarms
All criticism. Yes, I know you don't
Happen to love Valère, but still that won't
Stop you from marrying him. A husband grows
Acceptable sooner than you suppose,
For love's the fruit of marriage— Oh, I'm a fool
To plead instead of laying down the rule.
Enough of this! From now on you'll give way
To all my wishes. Listen and obey:
Your new fiancé will be coming here
This evening; I expect you to appear
Grateful and gracious, with a smile that tells
Plainly how much you welcome him. Or else—

[*He goes out.*]

LISETTE: What's all your demonstration of dismay for?
This is what most young ladies like you pray for.
When Father mentions marriage they reply
"Yes" on the spot. They certainly don't cry.
If someone came to me and said, "I insist
On giving you this man," would I resist?
Instead of looking mortified, my guess is
I'd rattle off at least a dozen yesses.
Your brother's tutor, who is far from dense,
Last week was saying something that makes sense:
"Women are ivy—" No, he wasn't bluffing—
"Pull it away from tree trunks and it's nothing.
Separate women from their men and they're finished
Just the same way; they're useless and diminished."
I can confirm his words. They're true to life,
And borne out by my experience as a wife.
God took my husband from me, as you know.
While he was still alive some years ago
You should have seen me: young and gay and fresh,
Rosy complexion, sparkling eyes, firm flesh.
Now look! I've turned into my own godmother.

Why, to keep warm at night I have to smother
Myself in blankets. But I well remember
How I could fall asleep in mid-December
Without a fire. Take my word for it, men
Are what you need in bed beside you when
The winter breaks, or to give you a squeeze
And say "God bless you" every time you sneeze.

CÉLIE: How can you tell me to betray Lélie
And break my vow? What will he think of me?

LISETTE: Lélie's an idiot for staying abroad
So long, if you ask me. I find it odd
That you don't hear from him. Why not be smart
And realize he's had a change of heart?

[CÉLIE *shows her a miniature portrait of*
LÉLIE *in a locket.*]

CÉLIE: That I will not believe. There isn't a trace
Of falsehood in his soul or in his face.
This noble mouth, this brow, this honest eye—
How could I think that they would ever lie?

LISETTE: He does look faithful and sincere, it's true.
Maybe you're right to love him as you do.

CÉLIE: And yet I can't—

[*The locket slips out of her hand.*]

Help me—

LISETTE: You've dropped the painting.
Madame, stand up, you've slumped! Good heavens,
    she's fainting!
Quick, someone, anyone!

[SGANARELLE *comes in.*]

SGANARELLE: I heard a call.
What's wrong?

LISETTE: My lady's dying.

SGANARELLE: Is that all?
The way you screamed I thought it must be serious.

[*He approaches* CÉLIE.]

Woman, wake up! Are you dead or just delirious?
She doesn't answer.

LISETTE: I'll bring back some water
And people to assist, while you support her.

> [SGANARELLE *holds* CÉLIE *up with one
> hand and feels for her heart with the
> other.*]

SGANARELLE: She's cold all over. I'm afraid it's death.
Wait—first I ought to listen for her breath.

> [*He puts his face close to* CÉLIE's, *as his
> wife,* MARTINE, *looks out of the window
> of their house.*]

I'm not a doctor but I'd almost swear
She's breathing still.

MARTINE: [*at the window*] What's going on out there?
My husband's in her arms! It's vice, it's lechery—
I'll run down and surprise him at his treachery.

> [*She disappears from the window.*]

[LISETTE *returns with two servants.*]

SGANARELLE: Let's hurry off for help; she's almost gone.
It's wrong of her to let herself pass on
And try to make it to a higher sphere
When everything's so nicely set up here.

> [*The* SERVANTS *take* CÉLIE's *arms and
> legs and march off, with* SGANARELLE
> *giving the orders.* LISETTE *follows them.*]

[MARTINE *comes out of the house.*]

MARTINE: No sign of him. I call it animosity
To flit like that and foil my curiosity.
Now I'm convinced he's up to something—what?
The little that I saw explains a lot.
At last I understand the freezing glances
I get in answer to my chaste advances.
He's saving his embraces for some younger
Acquaintances while I, poor woman, hunger.
They're all alike, these husbands in captivity:
Give them their freedom and they take a liberty.
In the beginning they're all steam and fire,
Kisses and poetry. But soon they tire
And leave us on our own. It's obvious

They're giving others what belongs to us.
Let's modify the law till it allows
A wife to change her husband like a blouse.
That would be wonderful, and quite a few
Other abandoned wives would like it too.
              [*She notices* CÉLIE's *locket and picks it up.*]
What's this? A jewel case from someone's pocket,
Carved and enameled—charming!
                        [*She discovers the catch.*]
                              No, a locket.
I'll look inside.

              [SGANARELLE *returns, talking to himself.*]

SGANARELLE: Dead? Ha! She had a spell
Of weakness; in five minutes she was well.
Is that my wife?

                        [MARTINE *opens the locket.*]

MARTINE: A miniature, how neat!
He's handsome, and the painting's very sweet.

SGANARELLE: What's that she's looking at?
                        [*He peers over her shoulder.*]
                              Upon my soul,
A portrait. I don't like this rigmarole.
An ugly thought has struck me, a suspicion—

MARTINE: [*still without seeing him*] The workmanship's a marvel
    of precision.
Some lady got this gift and now she's missing it.
It smells so fragrant, too.

SGANARELLE: Good God, she's kissing it!
At last I follow—

MARTINE: [*aloud*]   Oh, it must be ravishing
To have a man so bold and brilliant lavishing
Attentions on you, bending to your whim.
I could be tempted by the likes of him.
Why don't I have a husband of this stamp,
In place of my old, hulking brute?

SGANARELLE: [*Snatching the locket away*]   You tramp!
I find you standing right outside our house,

Dismantling the honor of your spouse,
And gather from your language that you drew
The wrong card; I'm not good enough for you.
Well, by Beelzebub—who ought to carry
You off—pray, what would you prefer to marry?
A more upstanding man than I? Unthinkable.
A straighter carriage? Spirits more unsinkable?
A loftier brow with thicker hair above?
A face and shape more clearly made for love?
I, for whom gorgeous women pant and sigh—
Thousands of them—I cannot satisfy
Your greed? But no, I'm only soup or fish,
An appetizer for the second dish.

MARTINE: I understand this bragging and abuse.
You think you can pretend——

SGANARELLE: Stop, no excuse!
The thing's here in my hand. No lawyer needs
More damning evidence of your misdeeds.

MARTINE: I warn you, don't provoke me any more
By adding trumped-up insults to the score.
I'm keeping tabs on you. But first I'll take
My locket back, and then you can——

SGANARELLE: Can break
Your neck! I wish I had *him* in my clutch,
And not his picture.

MARTINE: What for?

SGANARELLE: Nothing much,
My lamb. I have no reason to complain.
I thank you from the bottom of my pain.

               [*He examines the portrait of* LÉLIE.]
So here he is, the darling of the bed,
The spark that lights your hidden flame, the head
That topples hearts, the urchin who——

MARTINE: Does what?

SGANARELLE: The wretch, I say, who— No, I'd better not.

MARTINE: Why does this drunken nitwit rage and shout?

SGANARELLE: Slut, you know very well. If this gets out
I'll lose the name I've always proudly borne.

Kids on the street will call me Mister Horn.
I ought to thrash you without hesitation
If only to uphold my reputation.

MARTINE: How can you rant like this in front of neighbors?

SGANARELLE: How can you revel in these randy capers?

MARTINE: What capers? Please inform me. Be explicit.

SGANARELLE: It's plain as day. I wish I could dismiss it
And smile courageously, as if it were a gag
To wear a pair of antlers like a stag.

MARTINE: First you insult me with the worst offense
A man can perpetrate. Then you incense
Me more by acting angry and by starting
To invent affairs that *I* have taken part in!
How fitting for the uncrowned king of knaves
To tell his spotless wife she misbehaves!

SGANARELLE: Impudent woman, when you play it haughty
No one would ever think that you were naughty.

MARTINE: Go, truckle to your mistresses, caress them,
Promise them pleasure, worship them, possess them.
But don't attempt to toy with me. That's mine.
                   [*She snatches the locket and runs off.*]

SGANARELLE: I'll get it back— I'll make her toe the line—
                   [*He rushes after her.*]

[LÉLIE *appears with his valet,* GROS-RENÉ.]

GROS-RENÉ: Now that we're safely home, I'm wondering,
Monsieur, if you'll explain one little thing.

LÉLIE: What is it?

GROS-RENÉ: Are you made of stone or steel
Not to give way after that long ordeal?
For seven days we rode the clock around
And almost drove our nags into the ground.
It's shaken me so badly that I feel
As if I've had a session on the wheel,
And that's not counting all the aches and tension
In one part of the body I won't mention.

Yet here you are, alert and looking bright,
Without a wink of sleep, without a bite.

LÉLIE: The ride was worth the effort. I've been dreading
The news since I was warned about the wedding.
I love Célie so much I must discover
How strong her feelings are for this new lover.

GROS-RENÉ: Yes, but to get you in the proper mood
To check on her you need a plate of food
Inside you. Then, Sir, if the news is bleak
It won't be such a strain on your physique.
I find myself that when I haven't eaten
The slightest misadventure leaves me beaten.
But when I've had a decent meal, together
With something wet to wash it down, I weather
The roughest storms of destiny. So stuff
Your stomach, Sir; too much is not enough.
And if you want to shut out troubles, line
Your heart with twenty brimming mugs of wine.

LÉLIE: I don't want anything.   .

GROS-RENÉ: [*aside*]   I'm getting thinner
Each second. [*to* LÉLIE] Can't I order you some
dinner?

LÉLIE: Not now.

GROS-RENÉ: My master's rules are so unjust.

LÉLIE: I'm worried sick; I couldn't eat a crust.

GROS-RENÉ: I'm worried *and* I'm famished—this affair
Is getting to be more than we can bear.

LÉLIE: Then leave me to myself. Don't be a pest.
Go off and gorge your fill and take a rest.

GROS-RENÉ: My master's rules, I say, are so enlightened.

[*He hurries away.*]

LÉLIE: I ought to look for her, but I'm too frightened.
She seemed in love with me and gave her hand;
Her father promised; I don't understand—

[SGANARELLE *reenters, triumphantly waving the
locket.*]

SGANARELLE: I got it back, and now I can inspect
The picture of this ugly dog who's wrecked
My wife and life—

> [*He squints at the portrait.*]

Don't know him.

LÉLIE: [*aside*]   How   did   he
Come by that souvenir I gave Célie?

SGANARELLE: [*commiserating eloquently with himself*]
Poor Sganarelle, your dignity's been dirtied
Too badly for it to be reasserted.

> [*He finds a certain pleasure in his sorrow,
> until he notices* LÉLIE *watching him, and
> draws away.*]

LÉLIE: [*aside*] Before I left she took that gift to serve as
A pledge of love. I've reason to be nervous.

SGANARELLE: [*aside*] My name will be immortalized in verse
As Sganarelle the Steer, or even worse.
The world will point two fingers in my face
To show how !owborn women bring disgrace.

LÉLIE: [*aside*] I could be wrong.

SGANARELLE: [*aside*]   Destroyed   before   my   time—
Oh, Jezebel, you've soiled me in my prime!
A monkey-featured juvenile has marred
My splendid image; I'm forever scarred.

LÉLIE: [*aside, staring at the locket*]
No, I'm correct; it is the portrait of me.

> [SGANARELLE *turns his back on* LÉLIE *and
> moves away.*]

SGANARELLE: [*aside*] He's watching.

LÉLIE: [*aside*]   Now I'm sure she doesn't
love me.

SGANARELLE: [*aside*] What does he want?

LÉLIE: [*aside*]   I have to get this straight.
[*aloud*] Pardon me, but I'd like to speak—

SGANARELLE: Too late.

> [*He starts to run.* LÈLIE *stops him.*]

LÉLIE: I'm curious to know how you acquired
                  That portrait, which I noticed you admired.

                            [SGANARELLE *looks at the painting, then*
                            at LÉLIE, *more closely at the painting,*
                            and finally at LÈLIE *from a few inches*
                            away.]

SGANARELLE: [*aside*] He's curious, is he? So is his request.
                  But now I think I see what's on his chest.
                  No wonder he was anxious to converse:
                  He's *it*—or to be accurate, he's *hers.*

LÉLIE: Would you be kind enough to tell me where——

SGANARELLE: I understand your question, and I share
                  Your trying circumstances, in more ways
                  Than one. This portrait of you—I must praise
                  Its likeness—came from somebody you knew
                  Immoderately well, a lady who
                  Cannot contain herself. And though she must
                  Have mentioned you, your deeds were not discussed.
                  But, to be frank, I wish you would refrain
                  From seeing her and putting such a strain
                  Upon the sacred bonds of marriage, for——

LÉLIE: You mean that you're her husband, and she's your——

SGANARELLE: My wife, exactly. Thanks for your acumen.

LÉLIE: My God, her husband!

SGANARELLE: Yes, I'm only human:
                  I like my marriage. Now, if you'll excuse me,
                  I'll tell her father.

                                      [*He goes off.*]

LÉLIE: How could she refuse me
                  And pick this lumpy creature in my place?
                  The rumors did him justice. Can she face
                  The memory of when we swore that oath
                  Of loyalty? Did it apply to both,
                  Or only one of us? I ought to fight
                  To win her back, if only out of spite.
                  The vixen— But this outrage to my pride,
                  Combined with the exhaustion of the ride,
                  Comes like a blow, a wave of violence breaking
                  Upon me, and I feel my body shaking.

[MARTINE *returns.*]

MARTINE: Monsieur, you haven't seen— But you're unwell.
It's lucky I arrived; you almost fell.

LÉLIE: It must have been the shock, a sudden malady—

MARTINE: Will you accept a little hospitality?
Come in the house and rest; you don't look strong.

LÉLIE: You're very kind. I will but not for long.

> [*They go inside, just as* SGANARELLE
> *appears with his father-in-law,* DORANTE.]

DORANTE: I sympathize, my boy, with your dilemma;
But aren't you rather anxious to condemn her?
What you have told me so far hardly leads
Conclusively to proof of her misdeeds.
These lapses on her part—although I grant
It's hard to judge—as evidence seem scant.

SGANARELLE: You mean I have to catch her in the act?

DORANTE: Don't be too rash; investigate each fact.
You should discover how she came to get
This gift and if she ever really met
This man. Be patient, and if your impression's
Confirmed I'll see she pays for her transgressions.

> [*He leaves.*]

SGANARELLE: That's sensible advice. I should proceed
With care. It's not unlikely that I read
Too much into one incident, and feel
Too vividly; those horns were almost real.
As for that miniature that made me quake,
Who knows?—it may have even been a fake.
So, with an open mind—

> [MARTINE *appears at his front door, showing* LÉLIE
> *out and holding his arm.*]

Blood, death, and war!
The portrait doesn't matter anymore.
Here's the original, in high relief
And in my house.

MARTINE: [*to* LÉLIE]   Your rest was much too brief
To let you get your strength back; won't you stay?

LÉLIE: I'd better not, Madame. I have to pay
                A visit. But I thank you for your help.

SGANARELLE: [*aside*] His mouth's still full of gallantry, the whelp!

                                    [MARTINE *goes in.*]
                He's noticed me. He'll never dare to speak.

LÉLIE: [*aside*] How could she give herself to such a freak?
                No, no, I must be logical, and tame
                This pointless hate. He's not the one to blame.
                Rather, I'll envy him a love so rare.
                [*to* SGANARELLE] Oh, lucky man, your wife's be-
                                    yond compare.

                [CÉLIE *appears just in time to see him leave.* SGANAR-
                ELLE *does not observe her.*]

SGANARELLE: Well, that was clearly put. He didn't mix
                His metaphors or call a dozen six.
                The horns are coming back. I'm red with shame.
                [*calling out to* LÉLIE] Now listen here, you haven't
                                    played the game.

CÉLIE: [*aside*] I'm sure that that was Lélie I discerned.
                It's strange he didn't tell me he'd returned.

SGANARELLE: "Oh, lucky man, your wife's beyond compare."
                Better beyond my reach. It isn't fair
                To have to watch them practice this deceit.
                He's swept the woman off her wicked feet.

                      [CÉLIE *approaches, but waits for him to*
                      finish his tantrum.]

                Now what? Am I supposed to fold my arms
                And let him go, as though I had no qualms?
                At least, I ought to stamp upon his hat
                Or muddy up his cloak or knock him flat,
                And then appease my fury and my grief
                By warning everyone that he's a thief.

CÉLIE: [*to Sganarelle*] Excuse me, but I wonder if you know
                That man who left a little while ago?

SGANARELLE: My wife's the one who knows him, Madame, not I.

CÉLIE: You seem to be all agitated. Why?

SGANARELLE: Forgive me this unseasonable lament
                And let me suffer to my heart's content.

CÉLIE: But what, Monsieur, has made you so distraught?

SGANARELLE: If I'm distraught, Madame, it's not for naught.
                I challenge any man of any station
                To be more cheerful in my situation.
                Before you stands the model for all men
                Whose honor has been overthrown; but then,
                My honor hardly counts beside the shame
                Of having been deprived of my good name.

CÉLIE: How?

SGANARELLE: Let me speak with all respect, Madame;
                They've made a cuckold out of me, a ram
                With curly horns. Today, with my own eyes,
                I watched them at their furtive enterprise.

CÉLIE: The man who just——

SGANARELLE: Yes, that philanderer.
                My wife's in love with him and he with her.

CÉLIE: My intuition was correct. I guessed
                This secret visit meant some cruel jest
                At my expense. I trembled when I saw
                Him spin about at my approach and withdraw.

SGANARELLE: Madame, you're very kind to take my part
                So personally. Others have much less heart.
                Some people that I spoke to thought me soft;
                Instead of showing sympathy they scoffed.

CÉLIE: [*calling after* LÉLIE] No punishment I know is too severe
                For this abominable act, this sheer
                Dishonesty. Don't think that I'll forgive
                You for it ever. You're unfit to live.
                But could it happen?

SGANARELLE: Well, it did to me.

CÉLIE: [*still calling*] How can a man behave so villainously?

SGANARELLE: The darling girl!

CÉLIE: [*still to* LÉLIE]   For you, my evil friend,
                The flames of hell would be too kind an end.

SGANARELLE: That's telling him!

CÉLIE: To pay back faithfulness
And innocence in such a way!

SGANARELLE: [*with a sigh*]   Ah, yes!

CÉLIE: To lay a simple nature open to
Contempt and insults.

SGANARELLE: What she says is true.

CÉLIE: I'd say more, but it only makes my madness
Increase; I feel that I could die of sadness.

SGANARELLE: There, there, dear lady, don't lose your control
On my behalf; your torments touch my soul.

CÉLIE: [*still to* LÉLIE] I hope you don't imagine that these pleas,
These useless imprecations, will appease
My anger? Never! I intend to make
You suffer, and I know what steps to take.

[*She goes out.*]

SGANARELLE: May heaven protect that girl from every danger!
How moving when you come across a stranger
Who bleeds for you! Now, after that attractive
Display of wrath, I can't remain inactive.
No man should try to keep his temper down
Under such blows, unless he's but a clown.
I'll comb the city for this hangman's bait
Who, in provoking Sganarelle, tempts fate,
And teach the scoundrel with one deadly stroke
Not to make cuckolds out of honest folk.

[*He turns about resolutely and strides
away, stopping after about four paces.*]

Slow down! The fellow has a fierce, hair-trigger
Appearance; it suggests that he'd disfigure
My back as gladly as he did my front.
Oh, horns! Oh, whips! Oh, weapons big and blunt!
I loathe these curs who're quick to take offense;
What I prefer is peaceful men of sense.
I never fight, for fear of retaliation;
My greatest virtue is my resignation.
And yet my honor whispers, "Do not blench;

Be brave; insist on taking your revenge."
My honor—let it babble, let it buzz
Inside my head for all the good it does.
Suppose I play the warrior and launch
A wild attack, and suddenly my paunch
Is run through by a length of sharpened steel
So that the whole town hears my dying squeal—
Tell me, my honor, what will you be worth
When I'm laid in that damp, unhealthy earth?
So I conclude that honor gravely warps
My judgment: better a cuckold than a corpse.
Who cares about deception? What's the harm
In it? It doesn't wound your leg or arm.
A plague upon the fool who first inflicted
Honor upon mankind and then restricted
Its exercise to cuckolds with clean lives,
Rather than to their double-dealing wives.
Penalties are for criminals, and not
For innocent bystanders. Explain what
You would do, honor, if you were in my position
And saw your wife cut loose without permission.
It's time for somebody to call a halt
When she commits the crimes and I'm at fault.
The police, not I, should deal with this miscarriage
Of justice, this abuse of legal marriage.
Aren't there enough disasters that befall
The average man? I couldn't list them all.
Squabbles and lawsuits, hunger, thirst, disease,
Follow each other in an endless frieze,
The pattern of our troubled lives. And now
This extra nuisance rears itself somehow.
A false alarm? Of course! I shake my fist
At it; I stamp on it; it can't exist!
And if my wife's done wrong then let *her* cry.
When I've done nothing, why on earth should I?
In any case, I ought to feel consoled
By knowing that I'm made in the same mold
As all my fellow husbands, for the fact is
Adultery's an awfully widespread practice.
Isn't the wisest man, then, he who stifles
His rage, instead of fighting over trifles?

People may say I'm stupid but, good Lord,
I'd look *more* stupid dangling from a sword.

[*He lays his hand on his stomach.*]

However, I still feel the circulation
Of bile within my belly; the obligation
To have my own back burns in me once more.
Where is that crook? I'll even up the score.
Let him beware as I stir up new strife
And tell the world he's sleeping with my wife.

[*He goes out.*]

[CÉLIE *reenters with* GORGIBUS *and* LISETTE.]

CÉLIE:
Yes, Father dear, whatever you decide
Will suit me perfectly; you be my guide
And sign the marriage contract; I accept
Its ruling as my law. Now that I've kept
My former feelings in control, I find
That you have my best interests in mind.

GORGIBUS:
That's what I like to hear, that sort of talk.
I'll skip for joy— No, someone's sure to gawk
And grin at me; but how can I express
My pleasure, my parental tenderness?
Come here, my darling child; give me a kiss!
I don't see that there's anything amiss
In such behavior. Fathers should be proud
To kiss their girls, and never mind the crowd.
How well I brought you up: what tasteful breeding!
You've made me ten years younger just by heeding
My wishes.

[*He goes out happily.*]

LISETTE:
That's a turnabout.

CÉLIE:
I'll cite
My reasons and you'll say that I was right.

LISETTE:
It's very possible.

CÉLIE:
That rogue Lélie,
My so-called love, has been deceiving me.
He crept back home with not——

LISETTE:
But look, he's come.

[LÉLIE *approaches.*]

LÉLIE: Before we part forever there are some
Unpleasant matters that I have to broach.

CÉLIE: You dare address me, let alone reproach—?

LÉLIE: In case I've spoken out of turn, I should
Apologize. You've made your choice. It's good.
You're worthy of your husband, I don't doubt.
Respect his love and shut my memory out.

CÉLIE: Yes, viper, I'll *return* his love and treasure
The hope that that will give you great displeasure.

LÉLIE: But why this fury in your voice and eyes?

CÉLIE: And why this show of innocent surprise?

[*Enter* SGANARELLE, *armed to the teeth.*]

SGANARELLE: War, mortal warfare, battle, blood, and scrimmage!
Slay the poltroon who desecrates my image.

CÉLIE: Now do I need to answer and accuse you?
Look there!

LÉLIE: I'm looking.

CÉLIE: Doesn't that confuse you?

LÉLIE: Not at all. You should be the one to blush.

SGANARELLE: [*aside*] My rage is rising in a steady rush.
My courage, mounted on its mighty steeds,
Goes forth to fight. Arrh! There'll be fearful deeds
When we catch up with him, and Sganarelle
Dispatches him unmercifully to hell.

               [*He stabs and lunges with a sword and dagger.*]

Smack in the middle of his ribs I'll throw one.

LÉLIE: Who is your enemy, Monsieur?

SGANARELLE: Who? No one.

LÉLIE: Then why these weapons?

SGANARELLE: These? They're my protection
Against the weather, if you've no objection.
[*aside*] Now I must kill him; let me just be brave.

LÉLIE: What?

SGANARELLE: I said nothing.

> [*He punches himself in the stomach and slaps his cheeks to work up his anger.*]

> [*aside*] Coward, chicken, slave!

CÉLIE: [*to Lélie*] The sight of that poor creature ought to prey
On someone's guilt; that's all I have to say.

LÉLIE: It should indeed. I look at him and think
In wonder of how low a girl can sink;
How she can make a mockery of love.

SGANARELLE: [*aside*] Oh, for one gram of courage,

CÉLIE: That's enough!
I'll hear no more; you're insolent and cruel.

> [LÉLIE starts to move away aimlessly.]

SGANARELLE: [*aside*] See, Sganarelle? She backs you in the duel.
Muster your mettle, summon all your vigor—
More yet, my bully; swell up even bigger.
Now! Stab him where he's weakest, in the back!

> [LÉLIE *turns to reply to* CÉLIE. SGANARELLE, *who has been stalking him, wheels in another direction.*]

LÉLIE: You take each word I speak as an attack,
So I'll pretend I'm satisfied and voice
Nothing but admiration for your choice.

CÉLIE: Yes, I'm delighted too that it's arranged.

LÉLIE: Why not? Defend it since it can't be changed.

SGANARELLE: Of course she should defend it. Don't the laws,
Monsieur, prohibit actions such as yours?
If I were not a gentleman with more
Restraint than most, these streets would run with
gore.

LÉLIE: I fail to understand your question. How——

SGANARELLE: Please note these decorations on my brow.
Your conscience and your natural discretion
Should tell you that my wife is my possession.
You've traded on my reticence and tact;
That's not the way a Christian ought to act.

LÉLIE: Your fear, Monsieur, is foolish and unfounded.
But don't stop there. Continue it. Compound it.
I know she's yours, and far from being jealous——

CÉLIE: Traitor, how you invent new lies to sell us!

LÉLIE: What! You suggest that I could entertain
One thought that might give this poor fellow pain?
You really do believe that I'm a traitor?

CÉLIE: Ask him, ask him! He'll give you all the data.

SGANARELLE: No, please, go on. I love the way you cried,
Madame. It's good to have you on my side.

[MARTINE *comes back, looking daggers at* CÉLIE.]

MARTINE: I'm not the type, Madame, who bears a grudge,
Nor would it be correct for me to judge
Your motives. But I won't be brushed off lightly.
I see what's going on, and it's unsightly.
Your heart should have more noble a design
Than capturing the heart that should be mine.

CÉLIE: That declaration isn't very clear.

SGANARELLE: [*to* MARTINE] Slut, who invited you to interfere?
She came to my defense; don't persecute her.
You're only frightened that you'll lose your suitor.

CÉLIE: Madame, I cannot say I envy you.

[*to* LÉLIE]
Well, was I lying? Now you'll admit it's true.

LÉLIE: I'm more perplexed than ever.

LISETTE: I wonder if
We'll ever reach the ending of this tiff.
I've stood by patiently and tried to swallow
It down. The more I hear, the less I follow.
Perhaps I'm the one who ought to put things straight.

[*She stands between* CÉLIE *and* LÉLIE.]

Speak when I tell you to. You others, wait.
[*to* LÉLIE]
In simple language, now: how has she hurt you?

LÉLIE: I had no doubts at all about her virtue
Until I heard the rumors, then I sped

Back here at once, praying I'd been misled.
My overwhelming passion for her carried
Me home within a week—to find her married.

LISETTE:　Married? To whom?

LÉLIE:　　　　　　　　　　　To him.

LISETTE:　　　　　　　　　　　　　　To him?

SGANARELLE:　　　　　　　　　　　　　　　　To whom?

LISETTE:　Who told you that?

LÉLIE:　　　　　　　　　　Why, he did.

LISETTE:　[*to* SGANARELLE]　　　　　　I assume
That this is true?

SGANARELLE:　　　　　　　I only said I was
The husband of my wife.

LÉLIE:　　　　　　　　　　I thought, because
I found you with my portrait in your hand—

SGANARELLE:　Yes, here it is.

LÉLIE:　　　　　—And heard you reprimand
The woman it belonged to—on my life,
You said yourself the woman was your wife.

SGANARELLE:　[*pointing to* MARTINE] She is. Without that locket
　　thing, I swear
I never would have known of her affair.

MARTINE:　What, my affair? I stood there in the street
And found the locket lying at my feet.
A little later, when this man looked ill,
I made him go indoors to rest, but still
I didn't recognize him at the time.

CÉLIE:　I dropped the locket when I swooned, so I'm
Responsible, as things turn out, for all
The fuss.

　　　　[*to* SGANARELLE] You took me home, if
　　you recall.

LISETTE:　You see? You'd still be shouting, "Viper! Traitor!"
If it were not for me, the mediator.

SGANARELLE:　Did all this happen to us or did it not?
My forehead for a while felt really hot.

MARTINE: I'm not convinced yet that my premonitions
             Were altogether false. I have suspicions—

SGANARELLE: In that case, I propose a lasting truce
             Between us, in which I have more to lose
             Than you: let's trust each other to the full.

MARTINE: Agreed, but if you slip, beware the bull!
             [CÉLIE *and* LÉLIE *have been talking
             quietly.*]

CÉLIE: Good heavens, if this is true, what have I done?
             It's all my fault, the consequence of one
             Distracted moment. Thinking you had broken
             Your marriage vow and gone back on your token,
             I took revenge by consenting to a wedding
             Which I am sure to spend my life regretting.
             My father has my promise. I foresee—
             But here he comes.

LÉLIE: He'll keep his pledge to me.
             [GORGIBUS *enters.*]
             Monsieur, I have returned, as you will note,
             Still deep in love, still ready to devote
             Myself entirely to Célie and show
             That I am worthy of her hand. And so——

GORGIBUS: Monsieur, you have returned, as I well note,
             Still deep in love, still ready to devote
             Yourself entirely to Célie and show
             That you are worthy of her hand. And so——
             I'm at your service. My reply is no.

LÉLIE: Is this, Monsieur, the way you keep your oath?

GORGIBUS: It is, Monsieur; my duty makes me loath
             To break my word to Célie's new intended.

CÉLIE: Your word to Lélie was easily amended.

GORGIBUS: Daughter, you swore to me that you'd abide
             By my decisions and take me as your guide.
             Valère— But here's his father, come to make it
             Final about the wedding plans, I take it.
             [VILLEBREQUIN *comes in.*]
             Well, Villebrequin, what brings you without
             warning?

VILLEBREQUIN: New information, which I learned this morning.
It cancels our agreement, for my son,
Who was supposed to wed Célie, has done
What none of us who are close to him suspected:
For four months he has been the undetected
Husband of Lise. I can't annul the match;
She's wealthy and well bred, a splendid catch.
I've come——

GORGIBUS: It's ended perfectly, and we'll
Start reconsidering. Let me reveal
That long ago I said I'd give Célie
To this young man, who's rich in honesty
And other virtues, and I wouldn't dream
Of having any son-in-law but him.

VILLEBREQUIN: A handsome couple.

LÉLIE: Thank you. [*to* GORGIBUS] May
you thrive
For making me the happiest man alive.

GORGIBUS: We'll set the date, now everything's decided.

SGANARELLE: What man ever looked more of a cuckold than I did?
Yes, *looked,* for this example proves it's vain
To trust appearances, however plain.
When all the evidence as you receive it
Adds up to one conclusion: don't believe it.

CURTAIN

The Rehearsal at Versailles

L'Impromptu de Versailles tells much and hints at even more about the conditions—and specifically the strains—under which Molière worked as dramatist and comedian to Louis XIV.[1] The structure of the play is loose and the suspense is provided only by the deadline for the play-within-the-play that is being rehearsed. The real interest for an audience today, though, is the drama on several levels. No doubt Molière found it convenient to produce a play that depicted a rehearsal, since it was conceived and staged in one week and any dropped cues or other unprofessional behavior could be attributed to the casual nature of the play itself; it may also have served him as an exercise in writing what looked like impromptu dialogue and thus working with a more "realistic" setting, framework, and content than had ever been attempted before. But given this inherent realism, Molière turned it to his advantage. This was not merely a representation of a rehearsal; it was also a statement of Molière's theatrical beliefs; an answer to his critics; an opportunity for perfect typecasting, since the actors are either playing themselves or playing themselves *playing*; and a new kind of drama for French audiences. (Shakespeare had written rehearsals into *Hamlet* and *A Midsummer Night's Dream*, but never as naturalistically as this.) Incidentally, it allowed Molière to capitalize on his comic gifts by burlesquing the acting of his rivals at the Hôtel de Bourgogne, though these imitations seem a little like sour grapes, in view of his own inability to

[1] Although, as Jacques Copeau points out in his essay on Molière's comedy-ballets (IAC, Lyon, 1943), Molière functioned well under pressure, perhaps more effectively than he would have done without the royal "deadlines."

carry off a heroic part. With all this, the play is modestly written; Molière was a sound enough showman to know that personal spite on stage is displeasing to watch, and the temperance he exhibits was in contrast to the spleen of his rivals who said and published many wounding things about him, his family, and his troupe. In the play Madeleine Béjart and Armande urge him to uncork some return abuse; he resists this, and today we can admire his taste and reticence, just as the Court audience may have done at the first performance in 1663, and three weeks later the public, when the play was given at the Palais-Royal. Perhaps the most striking effect of the play comes after the sequence in which Molière plays an imaginary marquess who detests Molière, while another actor, Brécourt, states Molière's case. Molière is thus arguing against himself. He intensifies this scene when he shows Brécourt how to play the part; we then see Molière playing the part of Brécourt playing the part of the chevalier who is speaking in favor of Molière. Pirandello, the master of this kind of many-dimensioned writing, never invented a more complex situation, yet the direction of the play is plain throughout. We do not know whether George Villiers, Duke of Buckingham, had Molière's play in mind when, eight years later, he wrote The Rehearsal with his friends in order to lampoon the heroics of Dryden and other English seventeenth-century dramatists. But certainly The Rehearsal at Versailles became the ancestor of several subsequent French plays, including Anouilh's La Répétition (1950) and Pauvre Bitos (1956), and Giraudoux's glittering L'Impromptu de Paris (1937), in which Louis Jouvet and other comedians put the playwright's point of view directly to the public, much as Molière had done for himself 275 years before.

THE REHEARSAL AT VERSAILLES

L'Impromptu de Versailles

CHARACTERS:

MOLIÈRE, as himself and as a ludicrous marquess
LA GRANGE, as himself and as a second ludicrous marquess
BRÉCOURT, as himself and as a nobleman
DU CROISY, as himself and as a playwright
LA THORILLIÈRE, as a marquess who makes a nuisance of himself
BÉJART, as an officious character

MLLE DU PARC, as herself and as an affected marchioness
MLLE BÉJART, as herself and as a prude
MLLE DE BRIE, as herself and as a furtive flirt
MLLE MOLIÈRE, as herself and as a satirical society wit
MLLE DU CROISY, as herself and as a soft-spoken vixen
MLLE HERVÉ, as herself and as a mannered servant girl
SEVERAL IMPATIENT SPECTATORS

Scene: The palace at Versailles.

[*The setting is the King's private theater in the chateau at Versailles, where the play was first performed. The members of the cast consisted of Molière's theater company, named the "Troupe de Monsieur," in honor of their patron, the brother of Louis XIV.*

Molière has called his company together to rehearse a new play, still untitled, which is due to be performed in less than two hours, before the King, who commissioned it. The actors stand about on the stage in twos and threes, discussing their parts or trying desperately to memorize their lines. MOLIÈRE, BRÉCOURT, LA GRANGE, DU CROISY, MLLE DU PARC, MLLE BÉJART, MLLE DE BRIE, MLLE MOLIÈRE (*Molière's wife*), MLLE DU CROISY (*Du Croisy's wife), and* MLLE HERVÉ *are present. The atmosphere is confused, the talk and behavior are extemporaneous, even after* MOLIÈRE *calls everybody to order.*]

MOLIÈRE: Please, ladies and gentlemen! You're wasting time we can't afford. Is everybody here? Damn it, will you pay attention?

[*He reads the cast list.*]

Monsieur de Brécourt.

BRÉCOURT: What?

MOLIÈRE: Monsieur de la Grange.

LA GRANGE: Yes?

MOLIÈRE: Monsieur du Croisy.

DU CROISY: Hello?

MOLIÈRE: Mademoiselle du Parc.

MLLE DU PARC: Well?

MOLIÈRE: Mademoiselle Béjart.

MLLE BÉJART: What is it?

MOLIÈRE: Mademoiselle de Brie.

MLLE DE BRIE: What do you want?

MOLIÈRE: Mademoiselle du Croisy.

MLLE DU CROISY: What's the matter?

MOLIÈRE: Mademoiselle Hervé.

MLLE HERVÉ: Almost ready.

MOLIÈRE: These people will be the end of me. Listen, all of you, are you deliberately trying to make me lose my sanity?

BRÉCOURT: We can't help it. We don't know our parts. You're making us lose *our* sanities, forcing us to go ahead like this.

MOLIÈRE: Actors—impossible creatures to handle—

MLLE BÉJART: We're all here. What do you want with us?

MLLE DU PARC: What do you have in mind?

MLLE DE BRIE: What are we doing?

MOLIÈRE: We have our costumes on. Let's get ready to start. The King will be here in two hours; we can make good use of the time by blocking out the business and improving the readings.

LA GRANGE: How can we act parts we haven't learned?

MLLE DU PARC: I honestly don't remember one word I'm supposed to say.

MLLE DE BRIE: I'll have to be prompted from start to finish.

MLLE BÉJART: I'll have to hold my script.

MLLE MOLIÈRE: So will I.

MLLE HERVÉ: I have practically no lines to speak.

MLLE DU CROISY: Nor have I, but I won't be responsible if I fluff them.

DU CROISY: One hundred francs for anybody who wants my part.

BRÉCOURT: Flog me twenty times before I play mine.

MOLIÈRE: Look at the way you're all quivering over a few simple parts. What would you do if you were me?

MLLE BÉJART: Who feels sorry for you? You wrote the play; you're not afraid of drying up.

MOLIÈRE: A bad memory's not the only thing I'm afraid of. If the play fails, it's my failure. To stage a comedy for this kind of an audience is no joke. These are not easy people to amuse or impress. They laugh only when they feel like it. What author wouldn't tremble at facing this severe a test? I should be the one who wants to back out.

MLLE BÉJART: If you're nervous, it's your own fault. You should have taken the proper precautions and given yourself more than a week to put the thing together.

MOLIÈRE: How could I help it? The King gave me an order.

MLLE BÉJART: How? By excusing yourself respectfully. By explaining that it's impossible in such a short time. Any other author would have refused to commit himself so heavily. What happens to your reputation if the play goes over badly? Think how your rivals will gloat about it.

MLLE DE BRIE: She's right. You should have politely asked the King to excuse you, or to give you more time.

MOLIÈRE: A King expects prompt obedience; he doesn't like obstacles thrown up at him. He wants his entertainment when he asks for it; he doesn't wish to be kept waiting. As far as he's concerned, the faster it's prepared the better. We can't study our personal feelings; we're here to satisfy him, and when he gives us an opportunity we must seize it and do our best to give him pleasure in return. It's better to make a clumsy attempt than not to make an attempt until too late. Even if we don't entirely succeed it'll be to our credit that we complied with his orders. And now, please, the rehearsal.

MLLE BÉJART: How are we supposed to rehearse when we don't know our parts?

MOLIÈRE: But you will, I promise; not thoroughly, perhaps, but you do know what the play's about and you can improvise, since it's in prose.

MLLE BÉJART: Pardon me. Prose is even worse than poetry.

MLLE MOLIÈRE: May I say something? You should have written a comic monologue for yourself.

MOLIÈRE: Be quiet, my darling wife; you're a fool.

MLLE MOLIÈRE: Thank you, my precious husband. That's how marriage changes people. You'd never have spoken to me like that eighteen months ago.[1]

MOLIÈRE: Will you please be quiet!

MLLE MOLIÈRE: It's strange how a little ceremony can destroy a man's fine qualities. The admirer becomes a husband, and suddenly he looks at his wife with a different pair of eyes.

MOLIÈRE: Enough of this chatter.

MLLE MOLIÈRE: Yes, that would be my theme if I wrote a play. I'd explain away most of the faults women are accused of; and I'd dramatize the contrast between the crabbiness of a husband and the courtesy of a lover.

MOLIÈRE: Touché. Let's drop the discussion; we have more important things to do.

MLLE BÉJART: When the King asked you for a reply to the criticism of your other work, why didn't you write the play about the Bourgogne actors, which you've often described to us? It would have been perfect for this occasion. When the critics did their satirical portrait of you they left themselves wide open, and your portrait of them would be a much more accurate picture than theirs was of you.[2] They tried to spoof your comic acting,

[1] Their marriage had occurred, to be precise, twenty months before.

[2] The reference is to Boursault's *Le Portrait du Peintre* (*The Painter Painted, or The Counter-Criticism of Molière's The School for Wives*), which was to be staged the following day by Molière's rivals at the Hôtel de Bourgogne theater.

but they weren't imitating you at all, only the role you were playing, your makeup, and the mannerisms you adopted in trying to draw a comic character from life. But if you mock an actor in a *serious* part you'll come very close to mocking him as a man, because serious acting doesn't allow him to cover up his personal faults with ridiculous tricks and comic gestures.

MOLIÈRE: That's true, but I had my reasons for not satirizing the Bourgogne actors. Between us, I didn't think it was worth the trouble. Besides, we'd have needed more time to work out the idea. They perform on the same days as we do—Tuesday, Friday, and Sunday—and I can't have seen them more than three or four times since we settled in Paris five years ago.[3] I've caught only the obvious heroics and flourishes in their acting, and I'd need more visits if I wanted to portray them with any depth.

MLLE DU PARC: I recognized several of them immediately from your impersonations.

MLLE DE BRIE: Oh, I never heard those.

MOLIÈRE: They were part of a skit, a flimsy item I had in mind at one time, which might not have been very funny.

MLLE DE BRIE: Tell me about it; you've already told the others.

MOLIÈRE: We can't spare the time.

MLLE DE BRIE: In a couple of words.

MOLIÈRE: I was thinking about a comedy in which a playwright— I'd have taken that part myself—offers a script to an acting troupe that has just come into town. He says [*imitating the playwright*]: "Have you the actors and actresses to do justice to a work of art? For this play of mine is——"

And then one of the actors interrupts him: "Well, Monsieur, we have some men and some women who seemed acceptable wherever we appeared."

"And which one of you does the kings?"

"Here's an actor who's tolerably good at kings."

"What, that slim young fellow? Are you joking? A king ought to be big and bloated, the size of four men put together, swag-bellied and circular. A man who really fills a throne, not a well-

[3] In 1658. For the previous fifteen years the company had been traveling through the provinces.

built youngster. That's a mark against him already. Now let me hear him declaim a few lines."

Whereupon, the actor recites some lines from Corneille's *Nicomedes*. You remember the King in Act Two, scene one:

"I must tell you, Araspe, he has served me too well;
    Extending my powers—"

And so on, with just the right shade of natural feeling. But the playwright says, "What, you call that declaiming? That mumble? Without any stresses? Listen to me . . .

> [*He imitates the style of Montfleury, an*
> *excellent actor with the Hôtel de Bour-*
> *gogne troupe.*[4]]

"I must *tell* you, Ara*spe*, he has *served* me too *well;*
    Ex*tend*ing my *powers*—"

"Notice my stance," says our playwright, "and the broad gestures. And at the end of the speech you must thunder out the last line. That's how you win your audience. You rock them; they love it; they scream for more."

"Excuse me, Monsieur," says the actor, "but it seems to me that when a king is carrying on a quiet conversation with one of his officers he speaks in a personal tone, not like Satan addressing his minions."

"That shows you don't understand the theater," the playwright cries. "Talk the way you just did and see if you get a single clap. Let's try something different: a love scene."

So next, an actor and an actress do a dialogue from *Horatius,* between Camilla and Curiatus, in Act Two, scene five:[5]

CAMILLA: "My love, will you take part in this grotesque
        Affair without considering the risk?"

---

[4] In his printed stage directions Molière calls this actor "excellent." Montfleury was, of course, an enemy, a stout, king-playing, "throne-filling" performer, and Molière hams up the impersonation. According to John Palmer, Montfleury's exertions on stage eventually cost him his life. He was "described by his contemporaries as dying not of fever or the gout, as the doctors alleged, but of [playing Orestes in Racine's] *Andromache,*" while another tragic actor, Mondory, "burst a blood vessel and died of paralysis."

[5] *Translator's note:* I have taken this extract from my own published version of Corneille's *Horatius* (Chandler Publishing Company, San Francisco), which is written in half-rhymed pentameters. In the other translations of Corneille here I have resorted to an anapaestic tetrameter, which gallops in English much as the alexandrine does in French.

CURIATUS: "Yes, I will go with him knowing, as I do,
That, from his hand or from grief, I must die:
A soldier's honor becomes his own scaffold—"

They do it naturally and quietly, as they should. But the play-wright comes back with, "That was a mockery—worthless! Here's the way to get it across:

[*He imitates Mlle Beauchâteau, an actress with the Bourgogne troupe.*]

"My *love*, will you take *part* in this gro*tesque*
Af*fair* without consi*der*ing the *risk?*"

"Now do you understand?" the playwright adds. "Passionate but not overdone. She doesn't stop smiling—did you watch my face?—through the greatest afflictions."

Well, that was the idea, ladies and gentlemen. We would have dealt with all the actors and actresses in the Bourgogne troupe in the same way.

MLLE DE BRIE: I like it, and I recognized each actor as soon as you said the first line. More, please.

MOLIÈRE: Rodrigue in Act One, scene six of *The Cid*—

[*He impersonates Beauchâteau, another Bourgogne actor.*[6]]

"With my heart deeply pierced by this terrible thrust
I find myself called for revenge. Now I must
Uphold my old father's discredited name
By wounding or killing *her* father—that same
Dear lady I love—"

Or this one from *Sertorius*. Do you remember Pompey's speech in the first scene of Act Three?

[*He impersonates Hauteroche, another actor.*]

"The enmity reigning between our two sides
Shall never enfeeble the honor that rides

[6] These extracts from Corneille's works were probably intended to take digs at that playwright, as well as at the Hôtel de Bourgogne troupe. At the time Molière and Corneille were not on speaking terms, but Molière continued to produce Corneille's dramas with "natural" diction and gestures. The quarrel was repaired some three years later; in 1666 Molière staged *Agesilas*, in 1667 *Attila*, in 1671 *Titus and Berenice*. All three heroic plays were heroic failures. Later Molière and Corneille collaborated with Quinault and Lully in writing *Psyché*.

> Above these low hatreds, distorted, perverse,
> Which threaten our virtues and bring even worse
> Disasters upon us—"

MLLE DE BRIE: Yes, I recognize him too.

MOLIÈRE: Or how about this fellow?

[He impersonates another actor, Villiers.]

Oedipus, Act Five, scene two, when he learns the truth about his birth:

> "You tell me my father, Polybius, is dead.
> But why did you come with this news that I dread?
> Why *you?* Why the minister whom, above all,
> He trusted? The man who has raised me? My fall
> Seems imminent now—"

MLLE DE BRIE: Yes, I know who that is. But there are a few of them in that company you'd find it hard to imitate.

MOLIÈRE: No, they could all be mimicked, one way or another, if I'd studied them properly. But you're making me waste valuable time again. Let's concentrate on ourselves, please, and not get diverted by any more chatter. La Grange, are you ready? You'll be playing a marquess, and so will I.

MLLE MOLIÈRE: Marquesses again!

MOLIÈRE: Is anybody else as appropriate for the comic butt? The marquess is your clown in modern comedies. Just as in the old days you had a servant as your comedian, today you must have a foppish marquess to get the laughs.

MLLE BÉJART: True, you can't do without your marquesses.

MOLIÈRE: Now, you, Mademoiselle du Parc—

MLLE DU PARC: I'm going to be awful in this part, and I don't see why you always make me play a fashionable lady.

MOLIÈRE: You said the same thing in the last play, yet you pulled it off marvelously. Everybody said you couldn't have been better. You'll do it again, I promise you. You just don't realize how good you are.

MLLE DU PARC: How's that possible? Nobody is less of a fashionable lady than I am.

MOLIÈRE: Exactly. That proves what a fine actress you are, capturing a person who is totally unlike you.

Now, I want you all to get inside your characters, to become them. Du Croisy, you're the playwright, and you must fill out his personality. He's a pedant moving in high society and trying to hold on to what he thinks is his integrity. Pompous tone of voice. Rigorous pronunciation which doesn't miss a single syllable; you can practically hear every letter spelled out.

Brécourt, your part is exactly the same as that of Dorante in the last play, an honest man at Court. Look thoughtful, speak in a natural voice, and gesticulate as little as possible.

La Grange, you don't need any advice.

Mademoiselle Béjart, you're one of those women who think that because they don't make love they can do anything else. They sit back proudly on their prudery, looking down on every newcomer, each one telling herself that other women's virtues don't compare with her miserable honor—which nobody wants to take from her anyway. Imagine her face in front of you so that you can catch the right expressions.

Mademoiselle de Brie, you play one of those women who thinks she's good as long as nobody knows she's bad. If there's no scandal, there can't be any sin. When she has an affair afoot she pursues it quietly, and she calls the young men who come wooing her "my innocent friends." Steep yourself in this character.

Mademoiselle Molière, you too will create the same character as the one in the last play. That's all I need tell you. The same goes for Mademoiselle du Parc.

Mademoiselle du Croisy, you're one of those people who pay nasty compliments to everybody; you never miss a chance to drop a sweet insult out of the side of your mouth, and you can't bear to hear anybody speak well of her neighbor. I think you can carry this off well.

Finally, Mademoiselle Hervé, you're similar to the servant girl in *Two Precious Maidens Ridiculed*. You join in the conversation now and again and borrow your mistress' jargon.

I've told you all about the important characteristics, and I hope I've impressed them on you. Now we'll run through the text and see how it goes. What's this? Someone has crashed the rehearsal; that's all we needed.

[*Enter* LA THORILLIÈRE, *a marquess who likes to be everybody's friend.*]

LA THORILLIÈRE: Good morning, Monsieur Molière.

MOLIÈRE: At your service, Monsieur. [*aside*] To hell with you.

LA THORILLIÈRE: And how is it going?

MOLIÈRE: Well enough, thank you. Now, ladies——

LA THORILLIÈRE: I've just been saying some nice things about you.

MOLIÈRE: You're very kind. [*aside*] Go up in smoke. Ladies, be careful——

LA THORILLIÈRE: You're doing a new play today?

MOLIÈRE: Yes, Monsieur. As I was saying, ladies, be careful not to——

LA THORILLIÈRE: And the King commissioned it?

MOLIÈRE: Yes, Monsieur. Ladies, you must watch out for——

LA THORILLIÈRE: What's the name of it?

MOLIÈRE: Yes, Monsieur.

LA THORILLIÈRE: I asked you what you're calling it.

MOLIÈRE: Good heavens, I don't know. Please, ladies, as soon as——

LA THORILLIÈRE: What costumes are you wearing?

MOLIÈRE: The ones we're wearing now. I'd like you all to——

LA THORILLIÈRE: How soon will you begin?

MOLIÈRE: As soon as the King comes. [*aside*] One stupid question breeds another.

LA THORILLIÈRE: How soon will that be?

MOLIÈRE: May I choke with anger, Monsieur, if I know.

LA THORILLIÈRE: You have no idea?

MOLIÈRE: Now look, Monsieur, I'm the most ignorant man in the world. I swear I have no reply to whatever question you ask me. [*aside*] I'm losing the little self-control I have left. This dolt wanders in with his pointless queries; nothing ruffles him, and he doesn't seem to realize that other people have work to do.

LA THORILLIÈRE: Ladies, your bewitched servant.

MOLIÈRE: Now he's starting on them.

LA THORILLIÈRE: [*to* MLLE DU CROISY] There you stand, as beautiful as a freshly minted angel. [*to* MLLE HERVÉ] Are you both in the play?

MLLE DU CROISY: Yes, Monsieur.

LA THORILLIÈRE: Without the two of you, the show wouldn't amount to much.[7]

MOLIÈRE: [*to the women*] Get rid of him. Shake him off.

MLLE DE BRIE: Monsieur, we're in the middle of a rehearsal.

LA THORILLIÈRE: Of course you are. Don't let me stop you. Keep it up.

MLLE DE BRIE: But——

LA THORILLIÈRE: No, I insist. I'm the last man to interrupt anybody. On with the show, as if I were not here.

MLLE DE BRIE: Yes, but——

LA THORILLIÈRE: I never stand on ceremony. You can rehearse as much as you wish.

MOLIÈRE: Monsieur, these ladies are trying to tell you that they prefer not to have any outsiders present during rehearsals.

LA THORILLIÈRE: Why? I'm not in any danger, am I?

MOLIÈRE: It's a tradition in the theater. And you'll enjoy the performance more when it comes as a surprise.

LA THORILLIÈRE: In that case, I'll run along and tell everyone you're ready.

MOLIÈRE: Don't hurry, please. There's no rush.

> [*But* LA THORILLIÈRE *scampers out with his news.*]

The world is full of fools. Once and for all, let's begin. You are all aware that the play takes place in the King's antechamber. That's a spot where amusing things happen every day. We can assume that almost everybody comes there, and invent reasons for the arrival of the ladies I've introduced. The play opens with the two marquesses meeting.

Remember to come in, La Grange, as I told you to, with that swaggering manner they call the society air, fussing with your wig and humming a little melody: la, la, la, la, la, la. The rest of you arrange yourselves over there to give us enough room; these are not men who let themselves be crowded in. First line, please.

LA GRANGE: "Good morning, Marquess."

[7] Mlles du Croisy and Hervé always played secondary roles; they were two of the less talented members of the troupe.

MOLIÈRE: That sounds nothing like a marquess. Take it a little higher. Most of these fellows affect a special way of talking, to distinguish themselves from the common herd. "Good morning, Marquess." Again.

LA GRANGE: "Good morning, Marquess."

MOLIÈRE: "Ah, Marquess, your devoted servant."

LA GRANGE: "What are you doing here?"

MOLIÈRE: "As you see, I'm waiting for all these gentlemen to move and clear the doorway, so that I can show my face."

LA GRANGE: "What a frightful crowd! I'm not at all anxious to join the crush. I like to be among the last to enter."

MOLIÈRE: "There are twenty people there who have no hope of getting in, yet they keep pushing and block every approach to the doorway."

LA GRANGE: "If we give our names to the usher, he'll call us in."

MOLIÈRE: "That's all very well for you. Personally, I have no desire to provide material for Molière."

LA GRANGE: "Yet I think, Marquess, that it was you he was imitating in *The Criticism of 'The School for Wives.'* "[8]

MOLIÈRE: "I? Excuse me, it was you to the life."

LA GRANGE: "Well! You're generous to lend me your characteristics."

MOLIÈRE: "No, you're funny to offer me what belongs to you."

LA GRANGE: "That *is* a scream." [*He laughs.*]

MOLIÈRE: "It's a *riot.*" [*He laughs louder.*]

LA GRANGE: "Do you seriously claim that you weren't the marquess in *The Criticism*?"

MOLIÈRE: "Of course I was; exactly like me. With that business in scene five about cream puffs. 'Cream puffs, I hate them, ugh! Cream puffs: they're detestable!' If it wasn't me, who else was it?"

LA GRANGE: "Nobody else. It's not a bit of use pretending to be ironic. If you like we'll bet on it and see which one of us is right."

[8] *The Criticism of The School for Wives* was Molière's previous play, and the one referred to during the casting scene ("You will be the same character as in the last play," etc.). In *The Criticism* Molière guyed some of the people who had found fault with *The School for Wives*; it is a tribute to the accuracy of his mimicry that everybody recognized everybody else as the butt of Molière's jokes.

MOLIÈRE: "How much?"

LA GRANGE: "I'll lay a hundred pistoles that it was you."

MOLIÈRE: "One hundred pistoles it was you."

LA GRANGE: "One hundred down?"

MOLIÈRE: "Ninety on account and ten down."

LA GRANGE: "Agreed."

MOLIÈRE: "Taken."

LA GRANGE: "Your money is taking a great risk."

MOLIÈRE: "Yours is in mortal peril."

LA GRANGE: "Who is going to settle this for us?"

[BRÉCOURT *approaches them.*]

MOLIÈRE: "Here's the very man. Chevalier!"

BRÉCOURT: "What is it?"

MOLIÈRE: Very good, Brécourt. You sound exactly like a marquess. But you're not playing a marquess. As I said before, I want you to speak naturally.

BRÉCOURT: I'll try again.

MOLIÈRE: Good. "Chevalier!"

BRÉCOURT: "What is it?"

MOLIÈRE: "We're engaged in a dispute over who is the model for the marquess in Molière's play. He bets I am, and I'm betting he is."

BRÉCOURT: "And I say it's neither one of you. You're both foolish to read yourselves into that play. The other day I heard Molière arguing with some people who charged him with the same offense. He replied that nothing displeased him more than being accused of taking particular people as targets. His aim, he said, is to portray types and not individuals,[9] and all the people who appear in his plays are imaginary, phantoms if you like; he invents them as he goes along, in such a way as to entertain the audience; and he would be embarrassed if they resembled actual people. For some

---

[9] Molière's naming of the actors he is imitating early in the play makes this speech sound less than sincere. He probably wishes to emphasize that he chooses to mock, not so much obnoxious people as objectionable habits and attitudes. All the same, his characters Trissotin and Vadius in a later play, *Les Femmes savantes,* seem to be satirical portraits of an abbè named Cotin and a poet named Ménage; and some of the doctors in his other plays are almost surely modeled on certain of Louis XIV's physicians.

reason, he said, his rivals always take a certain pleasure in tracking down mannerisms and attributing them to people he didn't think of at all, in order to spoil his relations with those people. It's become almost bad enough, he said, to deter him from writing any more plays; and I agree with him. Why bother to pin such and such a trait on so-and-so when his characters have traits that could fit a hundred different people? The business of comedy is to present the flaws common to all men, and especially the men of our time. It would be impossible for Molière to dream up people who resembled nobody you've ever met. If he is going to be challenged with pillorying every living person who has the same faults as his characters, he will indeed have to stop writing plays."

MOLIÈRE: "Come, come, Chevalier. You're defending Molière in order to spare our friend here."

LA GRANGE: [*to* MOLIÈRE] "You've missed the point. It's you he's sparing. I vote that we get some other opinions."

MOLIÈRE: "Yes. But first tell us, Chevalier, if you don't think that your Molière is running out of inspiration?"

BRÉCOURT: "No, my dear Marquess, I don't. We'll keep providing new inspiration, because that's our nature. We never change, whatever he says or does."

MOLIÉRE: Just a moment. Let's bring that whole section out more strongly. I'll run through the passage first. Listen:

"First tell us, Chevalier, if you don't think that your Molière is running out of inspiration?"

"No, my dear Marquess, I don't. We'll keep providing new inspiration, because that's our nature. We never change, whatever he says or does. Do you imagine that he has used up every human folly? Without going outside this Court, can't we think of twenty types he hasn't so much as touched on? For example, how about those who tear their friends apart—as soon as the friends move away? Or the sycophants who praise everybody they meet with the sort of sweetness that turns your stomach? Or those creeping characters who curry favor with you when you're rich and turn their backs on you the moment you're in trouble? Or those discontented souls, those useless hangers-on who grumble about other people's appointments when they've spent the past ten years plaguing the Prince for a post? Or those lickspittles who try to top each other with their servile greetings? — 'Monsieur, your most affectionate servant.' — 'Monsieur, I am entirely yours.'

— 'My friend, I would do anything for you.'

— 'Use me as you will, Monsieur; treat me as your dearest intimate.'

— 'Monsieur, I embrace you gratefully.'

— 'Ah, Monsieur, how I have missed you! Be generous and let me defer to your every whim!'

— 'Let me convince you that I belong to you. I revere you unashamedly.'

— 'I honor nobody more than you. I beg you to believe me.'

— 'I entreat you never to doubt my loyalty.'

— 'I am your lackey.'

— 'Your creature.'

— 'Your slave.'

"And so on. You see, Marquess, Molière has more subjects to choose from than he'll ever know what to do with. Add up all the things he has picked on so far and they're a mere fraction of what remains."

That's roughly how the speech should go.

BRÉCOURT: I follow.

MOLIÈRE: Take it from there.

BRÉCOURT: "Here come Climène and Élise."

MOLIÈRE: That's your cue, ladies. Mademoiselle du Parc, make certain you wiggle your hips correctly and exaggerate your behavior. You may feel uncomfortable, but what does that matter? Sometimes we have to do violence to our nice, normal selves.

MLLE MOLIÈRE: "Indeed, Madame, I knew it was you even from a distance because nobody else has quite the same walk."

MLLE DU PARC: "I'm waiting here for a man to come out, you know. I have some business to arrange with him."

MLLE MOLIÈRE: "The same with me."

MOLIÈRE: Ladies, you can use these boxes for chairs.

MLLE DU PARC: "Won't you have a seat, Madame?"

MLLE MOLIÈRE: "After you, Madame."

MOLIÈRE: Good. You nod greetings to the others and stay seated for the rest of the conversation. Not the two marquesses, though. They bob up and down—they stand, they sit—as they feel more or less agitated.

"Chevalier, you really ought to give your garters some medicine."

BRÉCOURT: "Why?"

MOLIÈRE: "They don't look well on you."

BRÉCOURT: "Thanks for not making me laugh."

MLLE MOLIÈRE: "Madame, I love the bleached white of your complexion and the angry red of your lips."

MLLE DU PARC: "Don't look at me, Madame, I beg of you. I am so ugly today."

MLLE MOLIÈRE: "Now, now. Lift your veil a little higher."

MLLE DU PARC: "I tell you I look frightful. I terrify myself."

MLLE MOLIÈRE: "But you are beautiful."

MLLE DU PARC: "I'm not, I'm not."

MLLE MOLIÈRE: "Do let me see."

MLLE DU PARC: "Please don't ask me."

MLLE MOLIÈRE: "Be generous."

MLLE DU PARC: "I dare not."

MLLE MOLIÈRE: "Yes, you dare."

MLLE DU PARC: "Why do you insist?"

MLLE MOLIÈRE: "A glimpse."

MLLE DU PARC: "Oh, why?"

MLLE MOLIÈRE: "I'm determined not to give up this opportunity."

MLLE DU PARC: "You're such a strange person. When you want something you want it feverishly."

MLLE MOLIÈRE: "I swear that you'll do yourself no harm by coming out into the daylight. Those awful people who tell me you put stuff on your face! Stuff and nonsense! Now I'll be able to say that it's not true."

MLLE DU PARC: "Oh, dear, I don't even know what you mean by *stuff*. Where are those others going?"

[*The others move toward them in a group.*]

MLLE DE BRIE: "Ladies, how would you like to hear some delightful news? Our dramatist, Monsieur Lysidas here, has just informed us that a play has been written attacking Molière, and it's going to be done by the Bourgogne troupe."

MOLIÈRE: "That's true. Somebody wanted to read it to me. A fellow named Basso or Broosso———"

DU CROISY: "His name is Boursault, and he is indeed listed as author on the placards, but I'll let you all in on a secret. A number of people had a hand in the writing, so now everybody's dying to see it. All the playwrights and actors in Paris look on Molière as their main enemy, so we united against him. Every one of us has added a brush stroke to the portrait, but we refrained from publishing our names. People would have thought it too easy if he were crushed by the whole of Parnassus at once. We want to make his defeat more shameful by giving the credit to an unknown writer."

MLLE DU PARC: "Nothing, I assure you, could make me happier."

MOLIÈRE: "Nor me. Mocking the mocker—just what he deserves. Now let him suffer."

MLLE DU PARC: "This will teach him not to make fun of everything. The scoundrel doesn't want women to have any wit. He condemns all our fine phrases and would like nothing better than for us to talk like cleaning women."

MLLE DE BRIE: "The language is nothing. He makes fun of our friendships, innocent though they are. According to him, it's dishonest to have any virtues."

MLLE DU CROISY: "That's unbearable. There isn't a woman in town who can do a thing anymore. Why doesn't he leave our husbands alone, instead of opening their eyes to matters they know nothing about?"

MLLE BÉJART: "That isn't important. The would-be wag satirizes even honest women; he calls them dignified she-devils."

MLLE MOLIÈRE: "I hope the rogue stews in his own juice."

DU CROISY: "He will, Madame, when the play is performed. The actors will need all the support we can muster."

MLLE DU PARC: "Let them not fear. I personally guarantee that it'll be a success."

MLLE MOLIÈRE: "You're right. Too many people have a stake in it. All those who think they have been mistreated by Molière won't miss the chance to come and applaud."

BRÉCOURT: "No, I can think of twelve marquesses, six *précieuses*, twenty coquettes, and thirty cuckolds who will come and cheer themselves hoarse."

MLLE MOLIÈRE: "I don't blame them. Why should he insult so many people, especially the cuckolds? Without them society couldn't function."

MOLIÈRE: "By heavens, I believe he and his plays are in for more than a painting—a pasting—from authors and actors alike, the greatest and the smallest."

MLLE MOLIÈRE: "Serves him right. Why should he write these wicked comedies for all Paris to see, with people in them we all recognize? Why doesn't he write like Monsieur Lysidas, who never attacks a soul? You never hear another playwright say a word against him. His works may not be popular, but they don't offend or provoke anybody and we all agree that they're elegantly written."

DU CROISY: "It's a fact that I've never been unlucky enough to make any enemies, and scholars seem to approve of my writing."

MLLE MOLIÈRE: "You can be satisfied with yourself then. That approval is worth more than the applause and the money that Molière's plays earn. What do you care whether or not the public comes to your plays, as long as your colleagues respect them?"

LA GRANGE: "When is the performance of *The Painter Painted?*"

DU CROISY: "I don't know, but I'm reserving a seat in the front row so that everybody will hear when I shout 'Bravo!' "

MOLIÈRE: "They'll hear me too."

LA GRANGE: "And me, by heaven."

MLLE DU PARC: "Just let any people boo and I'll drown them out. [*modestly*] It's the least we can do to uphold our interests."

MLLE MOLIÈRE: "Well said."

MLLE DE BRIE: "We're with you, every one of us."

MLLE BÉJART: "Definitely."

MLLE DU CROISY: "With all my heart."

MLLE HERVÉ: "No quarter for this reputation-ruiner."

MOLIÈRE: "My word, Chevalier, your Molière had better go into hiding."

BRÉCOURT: "Not he. If I know him, he'll be at the opening night and he'll laugh as loudly as everybody else at the caricature of himself."[10]

[10] This is, in fact, what Molière did during the first showing of *The Painter Painted*.

MOLIÈRE: "Yes, through his clenched teeth."

BRÉCOURT: "Who knows? He may find more matter for enjoyment in the play than you expect. I've looked at the script, and since the most amusing lines in it are lifted from Molière's own work, he won't object if the audience likes them. As for the remarks that are intended to slight him, unless I'm very much mistaken the audience will have no sympathy for them. And when it comes to the people who are gathering to support the play because they think Molière's characters are too close to real life, I can only say they're behaving in doubtful taste. I can imagine nothing more ridiculous. I never thought that it was immoral for an actor to imitate people skillfully."

LA GRANGE: "The Bourgogne performers tell me that they expect him to retaliate in some way, and that——"

BRÉCOURT: "Retaliate? If you ask me, he'd be a fool to bother. Everybody knows the motives behind this play and why it's full of invective; the best reply he could make would be to write a new play that becomes as much of a hit as the others. That's how he should take his revenge. And if I know anything of the Bourgogne actors, nothing will annoy them more than losing their audiences to his next production. It will be better than a thousand comedies that satirize them in person."

MOLIÈRE: "But, Chevalier——"

MLLE BÉJART: May I interrupt the rehearsal for a moment. I want to say something. If I were you, I'd arrange things differently. Everybody expects you to make a vigorous reply, and from what I heard of the way you were dealt with in that comedy, you have every right to come back at them; I hope you won't spare a single one.

MOLIÈRE: I get angry when I hear you speak like that. You women, you'd like me to fly off the handle and copy their cheap gibes. How much good would that do me? How much harm would it do them? Isn't that just what they're prepared for? When they were thinking about this play of theirs in the first place, they must have said to each other, "Let him abuse us as much as he likes afterward, as long as we make our money." Is it possible to shame such people? Won't I avenge myself better by *not* giving them what they expect?

MLLE DE BRIE: They made a great fuss, all the same, about those three or four words you used against them in *The Criticism* and *Two Precious Maidens*.

MOLIÈRE: It's true. Those three or four words were insulting, and they're right to quote them. But that's not why they're annoyed. The real injury I've done them is that I've been fortunate enough to make audiences laugh a little louder than they can. They've envied us for that ever since we came to Paris. But let them try whatever they wish; they won't disturb me. They criticize my plays? All the better! Heaven forbid that those plays should ever please them! I'd be most unhappy about *that*.

MLLE DE BRIE: Still, it's not much fun to see your works torn to bits.

MOLIÈRE: What's that to me? I got as much out of my play as I'd hoped for, because it appealed to the select audience at Court, for whom it was written. These insults have come a little late. But if they come at all, that's hardly my business now. It's not my play or the craftsmanship of it that is being attacked, but the King and his friends, who liked it.

MLLE DE BRIE: All the same, I wouldn't let that squirt of a Boursault get away with vilifying somebody who has done nothing to him.

MOLIÈRE: You're mad. Boursault as the theme of an evening's entertainment for the Court? How could you distort him to make him seem amusing? And suppose, somehow, that you could, he'd be grateful to raise a laugh, any laugh, even at his own expense. You'd be doing him too much honor to impersonate him in front of such a distinguished gathering. He couldn't ask for more. He's a man who has nothing to lose. He chooses to attack me because that is one way of getting his name known. The Bourgogne actors have unleashed him only in order to entangle me in an idiotic war, and to keep me so busy fighting it that I won't have time to write more plays. And yet you are simple enough to want to adopt their strategy! What am I going to do, then? Well, I intend to make a public announcement to this effect:

I will not answer their criticisms or their countercriticisms. They can say the very worst things of my plays; I don't mind. They can take my plays and turn them inside out like jackets for their stage, and they can try to profit from whatever good things they find in them and from my modest success; I give my consent. They need the material, and I am only too happy to contribute to their keep, provided they're happy with what I grant them. For courtesy has its limits; there are some things that don't amuse either spectators or the people who are being mocked. I willingly offer up my plays, my face, my gestures, my words, my tone of voice. I sacrifice my tricks of the trade for them to use as they will. I have no objections to whatever they take, if only the audience likes it. But in yielding all this to them I reserve the rest as my own property. They must be fair and not accuse me of moral or religious delinquency, as they have done in the past.

That is all I will politely ask of this honest gentleman whom they've engaged to write their play, and that is the only retaliation they shall have from me.

MLLE BÉJART: But in the end——

MOLIÈRE: But in the end you'll infuriate me. Let's say no more about it. We're chattering once more instead of rehearsing. Where were we? I don't remember.

MLLE DE BRIE: We'd just got to the place where——

MOLIÈRE: What's that noise? It must be the King coming, and now we have no time to go through the rest of the script. That's what comes of gossiping. Well, it's too bad. I can only say: do the best you can.

MLLE BÉJART: I'm so frightened. If we don't run through the whole play again, I'll go dry.

MOLIÈRE: You still don't know your part thoroughly?

MLLE BÉJART: No.

MLLE DU PARC: Nor do I.

MLLE DE BRIE: Nor do I.

MLLE MOLIÈRE: Nor I.

MLLE HERVÉ: Nor I.

MLLE DU CROISY: Nor I.

MOLIÈRE: What can I do? Are you all mocking me?

[BÉJART *enters.*]

BÉJART: Gentlemen, I have been asked to advise you that the King is here and is waiting for you to begin.

MOLIÈRE: Ah, Monsieur, I'm in torment at this moment, in utter despair. These ladies are terrified; they say they must rehearse their lines more thoroughly before we can perform. We beseech you; allow us a few more minutes. The King is magnanimous and he knows that we have been rushed.

[BÉJART *nods and leaves.*]

[*to the actresses*] Now, please! Try to pull yourselves together. Be brave.

MLLE DU PARC: You'd better ask the King to excuse you.

MOLIÈRE: At this time? How?

[*Some* COURTIERS *file in and take their places.*]

FIRST COURTIER: Gentlemen, let's begin.

MOLIÈRE: In a moment, Monsieur. [*to the actors*] I think I'm losing my mind over this——

SECOND COURTIER: Gentlemen, let's begin.

MOLIÈRE: One moment, Monsieur. [*to* MLLE DU PARC] And then what? Do you want me to affront the King?

THIRD COURTIER: Gentlemen, let's begin.

MOLIÈRE: We will, we will. [*to the actors*] All these people come busting in and tell us to begin, but the King himself hasn't given us the order yet.

FOURTH COURTIER: Gentlemen, let's begin.

MOLIÈRE: Very soon, Monsieur. What's this? He's coming back with the order?

[BÉJART *returns.*]

Yes, Monsieur, you've come to tell us to begin, but——

BÉJART: No, gentlemen, I've come to tell you that the King has been informed of your difficulties, and by his special grace has asked me to say that your new comedy may be postponed and that he will be satisfied with any other play you are ready to give.

MOLIÈRE: Monsieur, you restore me to life. The King has granted us the greatest possible favor in giving us more time to prepare the play that was written at his request, and he has our devout thanks for his boundless generosity.

CURTAIN

The Forced Marriage

With music composed by Lully, ballet interludes in which Louis XIV, the Duc d'Enghien, the Marquis de Villeroy, and other noblemen took part, *Le Mariage forcé* was first and foremost a Court entertainment. Its opening performance in January, 1664, took place in the Queen Mother's apartment in the Louvre. As though to assert that he was faithful to his early sources, Molière went back to what looks on the surface like another commedia dell'arte plot but actually owes a debt to Rabelais's dialogue between Panurge and Pantagruel. The former wants to get married for pleasure and companionship—*Vae soli* (Woe unto him who is alone)—but is afraid that somebody will make a cuckold of him, as he in his time has cuckolded others. After the first sequence between Sganarelle and Géronimo, Molière brings on Dorimène, and in the space of a few pages succinctly establishes these three characters and Sganarelle's dilemma. The play introduces five more characters, in addition to the two Gypsies, and each one occupies an important role in the story, yet is differentiated as a personality. For its length this is Molière's most neatly executed comedy. The philosophers, living in their tight little mental enclosures, undoubtedly inspired similar characters who later appear in *Monsieur de Pourceaugnac, Le Bourgeois gentilhomme,* and *Le Malade imaginaire.* It is worth noticing that in *The Forced Marriage,* as in many of his other plays, Molière does not spare his hero. The plot is rounded off logically at the end, but Sganarelle's destiny is not an enviable one. Unlike many of his successors, Molière refused to impose a happy ending by, for example, making his character see the light and save himself through good resolutions. One often feels that an extra act could be written to many modern comedies—this has even become a parlor game—in which the reconciled hero and heroine are becoming less reconciled and having third thoughts about each other. In Molière's plays the future is clearly determined and it looks black; laughter prefigures misery; but the misery is still to come.

THE FORCED MARRIAGE

Le Mariage forcé

———

CHARACTERS:

SGANARELLE, a middle-aged bachelor
GÉRONIMO, his friend
DORIMÈNE, his fiancée
ALCANTOR, her father
ALCIDAS, her brother
LYCASTE, her admirer
A SMALL BOY
FIRST GYPSY WOMAN
SECOND GYPSY WOMAN
PANCRACE, an Aristotelian philosopher
MARPHURIUS, a Pyrrhonian or skeptical philosopher

Scene: In a public square.

———

[*A street in Paris, outside the houses of* SGANARELLE, *a middle-aged bachelor, and his neighbor* ALCANTOR. SGANARELLE *is looking back from his doorway and calling out instructions to a servant inside. His friend* GÉRONIMO *stands close by, looking and listening.*]

SGANARELLE: [*speaking to someone inside the house*] I'll be back in a moment. Take good care of the house and keep everything in order. If anybody brings money, rush over to Seigneur Géronimo's house; I'll be there. If anybody asks for money, I'm out and you don't know when I'm coming back.

GÉRONIMO: [*overhearing* SGANARELLE'S *words*] That's a sensible order.

SGANARELLE: [*turning, surprised*] Ah, Géronimo, I find you here and here I was going to look for you.

GÉRONIMO: Any special reason?

SGANARELLE: To tell you about some business of mine and ask your advice.

GÉRONIMO: [*taking off his hat politely*] With pleasure. I'm delighted that we met. We can talk freely here.

SGANARELLE: No need to keep your hat off. Now—this is a serious matter that's been proposed to me and it's wise not to take any step without first talking it over with your friends.

GÉRONIMO: I'm honored that you've chosen me. What is it all about?

SGANARELLE: Before I speak, I want to be sure you won't flatter me. Be blunt. Say what you think.

GÉRONIMO: If that's what you wish.

SGANARELLE: There's nothing worse than a friend who won't speak his mind openly.

GÉRONIMO: Correct.

SGANARELLE: These days it's hard enough to find a sincere friend.

GÉRONIMO: That's true.

SGANARELLE: Géronimo, promise you'll give me a frank answer.

GÉRONIMO: I promise.

SGANARELLE: Take an oath on it.

GÉRONIMO: I swear by our friendship. Just tell me what it is.

SGANARELLE: [*cautiously*] In your opinion, should I get married?

GÉRONIMO: You? Married?

SGANARELLE: Yes, I, in the first person single. What do you say?

GÉRONIMO: First, tell me one thing.

SGANARELLE: What's that?

GÉRONIMO: How old are you?

SGANARELLE: Old?

GÉRONIMO: Yes.

SGANARELLE: How would I know? Whatever I am, I'm fit for my age.

GÉRONIMO: Don't you even know how old you are? Roughly?

SGANARELLE: Is that all I have to think about?

GÉRONIMO: Listen, how old were you when we first met?

SGANARELLE: I couldn't have been more than twenty.

GÉRONIMO: How long were we together in Rome?

SGANARELLE: Eight years.

GÉRONIMO: How long did you live in England?

SGANARELLE: Seven years.

GÉRONIMO: And later in Holland?

SGANARELLE: Five and a half years.

GÉRONIMO: How long is it since you came back here?

SGANARELLE: That was in 'fifty-six.

GÉRONIMO: From 'fifty-six to 'sixty-eight[1]—that's twelve years, isn't it? Five years in Holland makes seventeen; seven in England is twenty-four, plus eight in Rome is thirty-two; and the twenty you had to start with—altogether fifty-two. By your own admission, Sganarelle, you're in your fifty-second or fifty-third year.

SGANARELLE: It's not possible.

GÉRONIMO: But you can't argue with the figures. And that's why I am going to speak as a friend, and frankly, as you made me promise I would. Marriage is not for you. It's a matter that young people should think about very carefully. But people of our age shouldn't think about it at all. If the greatest folly in life is to get married, the greatest disaster is to do so during our autumn years, by which time we should have grown wiser. Here, then, is my advice: don't even *consider* marriage. You'll become a public laughingstock if you deliberately take up those heavy chains after remaining free of them for so long.

SGANARELLE: I have only one reply to make to that: I am determined to get married, in spite of everything you say. And there's no danger whatever of my being a laughingstock if I marry this particular girl.

GÉRONIMO: There's a particular girl? You didn't tell me that.

SGANARELLE: A girl I happen to like. A girl I happen to love with my whole heart.

GÉRONIMO: I see—with your whole heart.

SGANARELLE: Yes, indeed. I've asked her father for her hand.

GÉRONIMO: I see—her hand.

[1] 1668 was the year when the play was published.

SGANARELLE: And what's more the wedding is this evening.

GÉRONIMO: For heaven's sake, get married. I won't say another word.

SGANARELLE: What, am I supposed to wreck my plans because of you and your idiotic advice? Am I no longer capable of dreaming about a woman? Let's not argue about how old I may be. Can you think of a man of thirty who looks fresher and more vigorous than I do? Isn't every movement of my body as snappy as it ever was? Do I need a coach or a sedan when I go out? Haven't I still got all my teeth—and very fine teeth they are too! Don't I still swallow four fat meals a day? And do you know anybody who has a more powerful pair of lungs than these?

[*He coughs a few times.*]

What do you say to that clean sound?

GÉRONIMO: You're right and I was wrong. Get married.

SGANARELLE: I used to dislike the idea. But now I have my reasons —strong reasons. Apart from the joy of owning a beautiful woman who'll lavish a thousand caresses on me, pamper me, and massage me when I feel weary—apart from that joy, I say, I must consider that if I remain as I am, the tribe of Sganarelles may vanish from the earth. By marrying, I'll be able to watch myself come to life again. I'll dote on those little creatures who've sprung from me, with their sweet faces—the spitting image of mine—skipping about the house all day, and calling to me, "Daddy, daddy" when I come home, and playing all kinds of delightful little tricks. I can already see half a dozen of them skipping around me.

GÉRONIMO: Nothing could be more enjoyable. Get married as fast as you can.

SGANARELLE: Honestly? Is that what you advise?

GÉRONIMO: I mean it. You couldn't do better.

SGANARELLE: You're a true friend, Géronimo. I'm very fond of your advice.

GÉRONIMO: What is the name of your intended?

SGANARELLE: Dorimène.

GÉRONIMO: Not that young Dorimène, the stylish, very pretty child?

SGANARELLE: That's the one.

GÉRONIMO: The daughter of Alcantor?

SGANARELLE: Yes.

GÉRONIMO: And the sister of that fellow Alcidas, who thinks of himself as a swordsman?

SGANARELLE: The same.

GÉRONIMO: Great God—

SGANARELLE: What's that you say?

GÉRONIMO: Good luck. Marry her right away.

SGANARELLE: Didn't I make a wonderful choice?

GÉRONIMO: The best. What a marriage! Don't wait.

SGANARELLE: When you say that, I could burst with excitement. Thank you again for your advice. Of course, you're invited to the wedding this evening.

GÉRONIMO: I wouldn't miss it. I'll wear a mask in honor of the occasion.

SGANARELLE: At your service, Monsieur.

GÉRONIMO: And yours.

> [*He goes off, choking with laughter as he speaks to himself.*]

Young Dorimène, the daughter of Alcantor—and Sganarelle, who is only fifty-three— Oh, what a marvelous marriage! Oh, what a miraculous marriage.

> [*He goes off, still laughing.*]

SGANARELLE: It must be a good match because it gives everybody such pleasure. All the people I've met laugh when they hear about it. I'm the happiest man alive.

> [DORIMÈNE *approaches, with a* SMALL BOY *holding the train of her gown.*]

DORIMÈNE: Boy, hold my train up properly. Stop tying knots in it.

SGANARELLE: [*aside*] Here comes my beloved. Ah, she is enchanting— That elegance! That figure! Could there be a man who'd see her and not long to wed her? [*to* DORIMÈNE] Where are you off to, Dorimène, my lovely darling, my dear spouse-to-be of your spouse-to-be?

DORIMÈNE: Going to do a little shopping.

SGANARELLE: [*circling her in admiration*] Ah, my pretty temptation, when I think of all those blissful years ahead of us! You'll do whatever I say, and I'll do whatever I please with you, and nobody else will interfere. You'll be mine from your top to the tips of your toes. I'll be the king of you—of your lively little eyes and your impudent little nose, your lovable little ears and your edible little lips, your dainty little chin and your bulging little breasts, and especially your— I mean, the whole of your body will be at my disposal, and I'll be disposed to fondle you as much as I like. Aren't you overjoyed at the prospect of this marriage, my precious plaything?

DORIMÈNE: Over-overjoyed, I swear. Until now my father has always held me in check. He's the world's worst tyrant. I've been raging to break away from him, so that I could go my own way, even if it meant getting married. Praise God you came along, and now I'm ready to make up for lost time. You're a man of the world; you know all about the fashionable life, so you won't be one of those narrow-minded husbands who want their wives to live shut up like bears in a cave. I could never face that. I hate being alone. I like games, visits, gatherings, open-air parties, and going out for drives. I adore every kind of pleasure. Think yourself lucky to have married a lady like me. We'll never quarrel. I won't check up on your activities, just as I'm sure you won't check up on mine. I believe that married partners should tolerate, not torment, each other. We'll have our own lives and our own friends, with not a breath of suspicion between us. I'll expect you to trust me, just as I expect to trust you. What's wrong? All of a sudden your face has gone pale.

SGANARELLE: Nothing, nothing. A few vapors in the brain.

DORIMÈNE: It's a common ailment these days. Once we're married, you'll never be troubled by another vapor. Now I must hurry away and get rid of these rags. I have to buy some decent clothes. I need quite a lot. Don't worry about it; I'll send the merchants to settle with you. Good-bye.

> [*She sweeps away, turning once to chide the* SMALL BOY *again.* SGANARELLE *stands bewildered.*]

[GÉRONIMO *reenters from the other direction.*]

GÉRONIMO: Sganarelle, I'm glad you're still here. I happened to meet a jeweler who heard you were looking for a magnificent diamond ring for your wife and asked me to tell you that he has one for sale, a beauty.

SGANARELLE: So soon? There's plenty of time for that.

GÉRONIMO: What do you mean? You were all excited before.

SGANARELLE: I've had a few second and third thoughts about marriage. Before going any further, I want to look into the whole thing more closely. I've just remembered a strange dream I had last night, and I'm wondering what it means. Dreams are mirrors, you know; they can tell us about the future. I seemed to be in a small boat on a rough sea, and——

GÉRONIMO: I'm in a hurry or I'd be happy to hear you out. Personally, I don't believe in the meaning of dreams. But if you want to talk this marriage over with somebody, try our two local philosophers. They'll be pleased to say everything that could possibly be said on the subject. And since they belong to different schools, you can weigh and compare what they tell you. As for me, I stick to what I said before. At your service.

[*He goes out.*]

SGANARELLE: He's right. I must talk to the philosophers about this situation.

[*At that moment,* PANCRACE (*the name means* pancratium, *a Greek athletic contest*) *appears. He is engaged in a one-sided dispute.*]

PANCRACE: [*shouting to someone offstage*] You're a Philistine, my friend. You should be banished from the republic of letters.

SGANARELLE: Good. Here's one of them, and he sounds ripe for a discussion.

PANCRACE: [*still shouting off, not noticing* SGANARELLE] And furthermore, I can prove by conclusive reasoning that you are ignorant, an ignoramus—no, an ignoramissimus. You are abysmally unacquainted with every single case and mode of the Aristotelian dialectic.

SGANARELLE: Somebody has crossed him. Doctor Pancrace——

PANCRACE: [*taking no notice of him*] You dare to attempt to debate with me when you're innocent of the very elements of debating logic!

SGANARELLE: He's too angry to notice me. Doctor Pancrace——

PANCRACE: Your proposition would be condemned by every breed of philosopher.

SGANARELLE: People shouldn't annoy him this way. I——

PANCRACE: You are as far from truth as heaven is from the earth.[2]

SGANARELLE: [*kissing* PANCRACE's *hand humbly*] Doctor, I come to you as a poor pupil——

PANCRACE: [*turning to him for an instant*] Your servant.

SGANARELLE: May I——

PANCRACE: [*facing offstage again*] Do you know what you have committed, you fraud? A false syllogism!

SGANARELLE: Please, I——

PANCRACE: The major premise is stupid, the minor premise irrelevant, and the conclusion ridiculous.

SGANARELLE: But I——

PANCRACE: I will never give way on this. I intend to uphold my opinion down to the last drop of my ink.

SGANARELLE: If I——

PANCRACE: Yes, I will defend my proposition hand and foot, tooth and nail.

SGANARELLE: Doctor Aristotle, what has made you so furious?

PANCRACE: [*turning to him and shouting into his face*] My fury is richly justified.

SGANARELLE: [*recoiling*] In what way?

PANCRACE: A man who is a stranger to all knowledge tried to sustain an erroneous proposition, a stupid, terrifying, detestable proposition.

SGANARELLE: May I ask what it is?

PANCRACE: Alas, Sganarelle, everything is upside down today. The world is fallen into corruption. Permissiveness reigns, and magistrates who were installed to keep order should blush at the intolerable scandal I am talking about.

SGANARELLE: What scandal are you talking about?

---

[2] Many of Pancrace's philosophical platitudes are spoken in Latin or bad Italian.

PANCRACE: Is it not a public shame, should it not be avenged by heaven, when a man has to endure the sound of an expression such as "the form of a hat?"

SGANARELLE: The what?

PANCRACE: I maintain that one must say "the shape of a hat," and not "the form." This is the difference between the form and the shape: the form is the exterior disposition of animate objects, while the shape is the exterior disposition of inanimate objects. And since the hat is an inanimate object, one must say "the shape of a hat," and not "the form."

[*He turns away to the wings again.*]

Yes, ignoramus that you are, there is only one correct expression, and that follows the terms laid down by Aristotle in his fourteenth chapter, "On Quality," of the *Metaphysics*.

SGANARELLE: I thought the world must be coming to an end. Doctor, just don't think about it anymore. I——

PANCRACE: I am in a rage. I am not myself.

SGANARELLE: Leave the hat and the shape in peace. I have something to ask you.

PANCRACE: [*turning away again*] Knave! Scoundrel!

SGANARELLE: I beg of you! Listen! I——

PANCRACE: Dolt!

SGANARELLE: Oh, dear. If only I——

PANCRACE: Trying to put a proposition like that to *me*!

SGANARELLE: But he's wrong. I——

PANCRACE: A proposition condemned by Aristotle!

SGANARELLE: I know, but——

PANCRACE: Expressly condemned.

SGANARELLE: You're quite right. [*shouting off*] Yes, you're a fool and a braggart. What, do you dare to dispute with a doctor who knows how to read and write! [*to* PANCRACE] That takes care of him. *Now*, will you please listen to me? I want to consult you about a personal decision. I've been thinking of taking a wife into my household to keep me company. The woman I've chosen is beautiful in every way. I'm very fond of her and she's in a passion to marry me. Her father has given his consent, but there's one snag: I'm a little afraid of becoming the—you know—the character nobody feels sorry for.

[*He indicates a pair of horns.*]

As a philosopher, what do you advise?

PANCRACE: [*shouting off again*] Before I accept an expression like "the form of a hat," I will concede that Nature does not abhor a vacuum or that I am nothing but a dunce.

SGANARELLE: [*aside*] A plague on the man! [*to* PANCRACE] Doctor, can't you listen to ordinary people? I've been asking you questions for the best part of an hour and you keep answering somebody else.

PANCRACE: I beg your pardon. I am consumed by a righteous wrath.

SGANARELLE: Forget about that. Just take the trouble to hear me out.

PANCRACE: What are you trying to say?

SGANARELLE: I must speak to you about this problem of mine.

PANCRACE: And which tongue do you intend to use?

SGANARELLE: Which tongue? The one in my mouth. I don't think I need to borrow the man next door's.

PANCRACE: That is to say, in which idiom will you speak to me? Which language?

SGANARELLE: Now I understand—

[*The following exchange is conducted at high speed.*]

PANCRACE: In Italian, for instance?

SGANARELLE: No.

PANCRACE: In Spanish?

SGANARELLE: No.

PANCRACE: German?

SGANARELLE: No.

PANCRACE: Latin?

SGANARELLE: No.

PANCRACE: Greek, ancient or modern?

SGANARELLE: No.

PANCRACE: Hebrew?

SGANARELLE: No.

PANCRACE: Syrian?

SGANARELLE: No.

PANCRACE: Turkish?

SGANARELLE: No.

PANCRACE: Egyptian?

SGANARELLE: No.

PANCRACE: Hottentot?

SGANARELLE: No, no, no! In the language we're talking now.

PANCRACE: I see. Very interesting.

SGANARELLE: Whew! Good——

PANCRACE: Would you please step around to my other side? The ear you are addressing is meant for scientific and foreign tongues, while this other one is for receiving our mother tongue.

SGANARELLE: [*aside, going to the other ear*] Talk about a performance with these philosophy characters—

PANCRACE: Now: your subject.

SGANARELLE: It's just a small difficulty.

PANCRACE: A philosophical difficulty, of course.

SGANARELLE: I'm sorry, but——

PANCRACE: You probably want to know whether Substance and Accident are synonymous or opposing terms in relation to Being?

SGANARELLE: Not at all. I——

PANCRACE: Or whether logic is an art or a science?

SGANARELLE: Not that, either. I simply——

PANCRACE: Or whether it takes as its Object the Three Operations of the Mind—Perception, Judgment, and Reason—or only the third, namely, Reason?

SGANARELLE: Hardly. I——

PANCRACE: Whether there are ten categories of Rationality or only one?

SGANARELLE: Not a bit. I——

PANCRACE: Whether the conclusion is the essence of the syllogism?

SGANARELLE: Not quite. I——

PANCRACE: Whether the Ultimate Good is achieved by instinctual desires or by disciplined behavior?

SGANARELLE: Oh, no. I——

PANCRACE: Or whether the Ultimate Good corresponds with the Ultimate End?

SGANARELLE: Not that, either. I——

PANCRACE: Whether the Ultimate End is an absolute or a relative value?

SGANARELLE: No, no, no, no! By every demon in hell, NO!

PANCRACE: Explain yourself, then. I cannot guess what is puzzling you.

SGANARELLE: That's all I want to do, if you'll only listen—

> [*At this point* PANCRACE *interrupts, and they start to speak at the same time.*]

SGANARELLE:

That problem of mine: This is what it's all about. I want to get married to a girl who is young and beautiful. I am very fond of her, and I've already asked her father for her hand, but I'm nervous, you see, because— (*He gives up; his temperature visibly mounts.*)

PANCRACE:

Man was endowed with the gift of the spoken word in order to explain his thoughts. Just as our thoughts are the portraits of objects, so our words are the portraits of our thoughts. But these latter portraits differ from the former portraits in that the former portraits must be distinguished from their originals, whereas the spoken word corresponds to its original, since it is nothing but thought externalized in signals; from which it follows that those who think clearly express themselves most effectively.

Very well. Now explain yourself to me by means of the spoken word, which is the most intelligible of all externalized signals.

> [SGANARELLE *gets hold of* PANCRACE *at this point and pushes him bodily into the house, shutting the door behind him and*

> *hanging on to it to prevent* PANCRACE
> *from getting out.*]

SGANARELLE: I can't bear it anymore.

PANCRACE: [*his voice floating out from inside*] Yes, the spoken word is *animi index et speculum;* it is the interpreter of the heart, the image of the soul.

> [*He appears at the first-floor window, still talking.* SGANARELLE *stands back.*]

It is a mirror that innocently reveals the most inaccessible secrets of our individual selves. And since you are blessed with the faculties of reason and speech, functioning simultaneously, why do you not make use of the spoken word in order to communicate your thoughts to me?

SGANARELLE: I would if I could, but you won't listen.

PANCRACE: I am listening. Speak.

SGANARELLE: [*taking a deep breath*] All I want to say, Doctor, is that——

PANCRACE: But above all, be brief.

SGANARELLE: I will——

PANCRACE: Avoid verbosity!

SGANARELLE: If you'll only let——

PANCRACE: Limit your discourse to a pithy maxim or two in the Spartan style.

SGANARELLE: If I ever——

PANCRACE: Out with it now! Enough of this circumlocution!

> [SGANARELLE *gives up and starts collecting stones to hurl at* PANCRACE *to break his head.*]

What's this? Instead of explaining yourself, you are moving away. You are more insolent than the creature I spoke to before who contended that one may talk about the form of a hat. I will prove to you in open contest, by demonstration and persuasion and unanswerable ratiocination *in barbara,* that you are not now, nor will ever be, other than a blockhead; and that I am, and will always be, *in utroque jure,* that is, in civil and canon law, the eminent Doctor Pancrace.

> [*He disappears from the window.*]

SGANARELLE: [*wound up to throw the stone in his fist*] The babbling chump!

[*He drops the stone.*]

[PANCRACE *appears at the door and comes out.*]

PANCRACE: I, Pancrace, a man of letters, a man of learning—

SGANARELLE: On and on—

PANCRACE: A man of achievement and the capacity for yet more— [*He begins to move away.*] A man schooled in all the moral, political, and natural sciences— [*He comes back.*] A scholarly man, a scholar among scholars, in every case and mode— [*moves away*] A man who has totally mastered fables, mythology and history— [*comes back*] Grammar, poetry, rhetoric, dialectic, sophistry— [*moves away*] Mathematics, optics, physics, metaphysics, prognostication, omination, vaticination— [*comes back*] Cosmography, geography, geometry, optometry, cosmometry, orthography, architecture— [*moves away*] Medicine, physiology, biology, astrology, astronomy, palmology, graphology, metoposcopy, chiromantics, hieromantics, geomantics—

[*He disappears. His voice is still heard faintly, reciting.*]

SGANARELLE: [*sitting down weakly*] Damnation take all these philosophers. They won't make contact with people. I was warned that his master Aristotle was nothing but a windbag. I'll have to look for the other fellow. He's more sober and sensible, I hear. Ah, there he is—

[MARPHURIUS *the Skeptic comes in.*]

Marphurius—

MARPHURIUS: What can I do for you, Sganarelle?

SGANARELLE: I need your advice on a small matter, Doctor. That's why I'm here. [aside] This one is better. At least, he pays attention to you.

MARPHURIUS: [*after a pause*] Sganarelle, I have thought about what you said, and you will have to change your way of speaking. Our philosophy enjoins us never to enunciate a decisive proposition, but to speak of everything with modest uncertainty, suspending our judgment. For this reason, you must not say, "I am here," but "I think I am here."

SGANARELLE: I think?

MARPHURIUS: Precisely.

SGANARELLE: But I think it because I am here.

MARPHURIUS: One thing does not necessarily follow from the other. You can think so without its being true.

SGANARELLE: What? Isn't it true that I'm here?

MARPHURIUS: It may or may not be so. We must doubt everything.

SGANARELLE: If I'm not here, who is this talking to you?

MARPHURIUS: I think that you are here, and it seems to me that I am speaking to you, but cannot be sure.

SGANARELLE: What the devil is this? You're making fun of me. Here I am and there you are and thinking or seeming has nothing to do with it. Let's drop these subtleties, if you don't mind, and continue with my business. I want to get married.

MARPHURIUS: I know nothing about that.

SGANARELLE: I'm telling you about it.

MARPHURIUS: That may be.

SGANARELLE: The girl is very young and very beautiful.

MARPHURIUS: That is not impossible.

SGANARELLE: Does it make sense or not for me to marry her?

MARPHURIUS: Either one or the other.

SGANARELLE: That's what I want to know. Marry her or not marry her?

MARPHURIUS: It depends.

SGANARELLE: Am I getting into trouble?

MARPHURIUS: You could be.

SGANARELLE: Please, a straightforward answer.

MARPHURIUS: I am trying to give you one.

SGANARELLE: I'm very attached to her.

MARPHURIUS: That might be understandable.

SGANARELLE: Her father has agreed.

MARPHURIUS: That is not unlikely.

SGANARELLE: But I'm afraid of becoming a—a cuckold.

MARPHURIUS: It could happen.

SGANARELLE: What do you think?

MARPHURIUS: Nothing is beyond belief.

SGANARELLE: What would you do, in my place?

MARPHURIUS: I do not know.

SGANARELLE: What do you suggest I do?

MARPHURIUS: Whatever you think best.

SGANARELLE: I'm losing my temper.

MARPHURIUS: I wash my hands of it.

SGANARELLE: You old fool! You thinker! You *seemer!*

MARPHURIUS: What will be will be.

SGANARELLE: I'll soon make you change your tune, you numskull.

> [*He seizes* MARPHURIUS' *stick and beats him all around the stage with it.* MARPHURIUS *squeals and cringes.*]

There's the fee for your useless advice. And now I'm satisfied.

MARPHURIUS: [*recovering*] You dare to attack me, to lay my own stick about my back, to beat me, a philosopher!

SGANARELLE: Marphurius, you'll have to change your way of speaking. We must doubt everything. You must not say I've beaten you but only it seems as if I've beaten you.

MARPHURIUS: I am going off immediately to complain to the police.

SGANARELLE: I wash my hands of it.

MARPHURIUS: I have wounds on my body.

SGANARELLE: Nothing is beyond belief.

MARPHURIUS: And you are responsible for them.

SGANARELLE: It's not impossible.

MARPHURIUS: I'll have a warrant made out for your arrest.

SGANARELLE: I know nothing about that.

MARPHURIUS: You will go straight to prison.

SGANARELLE: What will be will be.

MARPHURIUS: I'll show you—

> [*He stamps off, waving his stick.*]

SGANARELLE: Impossible to get a straight word out of him. You know as much when you finish as when you began. Where can I turn for advice? The wedding's coming nearer and nearer. Was there ever a man in such a plight before?

> [*Two* GYPSY WOMEN *enter, carrying tambourines, dancing and singing in rhythm.*]

Gypsies! Fortune-tellers! They can foresee my future. I like their spirit and passion and rhythm. Ladies, can you read my fortune?

FIRST GYPSY: Yes, kind gentleman, we're the fortune-tellers for you.

SECOND GYPSY: All you do is cross our palms with silver and we'll give you the information you want to hear.

SGANARELLE: Here you are, then.

> [*He gives them money.*]

FIRST GYPSY: You have a kind face, kind gentleman, a kind face.

SECOND GYPSY: Yes, a kind face—the face of a man who'll be something someday.

FIRST GYPSY: You'll be married shortly, kind gentleman, you'll be married shortly.

SECOND GYPSY: To a nice woman, kind gentleman, a nice woman.

FIRST GYPSY: A woman everybody will love and cherish.

SECOND GYPSY: A woman who'll make many friends for you, kind gentleman, many friends.

FIRST GYPSY: A woman who'll bring you wealth.

SECOND GYPSY: A woman who'll give you a great reputation.

FIRST GYPSY: She'll take care of you, kind gentleman, she'll take care of you.

SGANARELLE: Now, that's all very nice. But tell me one thing: will I become a cuckold?

SECOND GYPSY: A cuckold?

SGANARELLE: A cuckold.

FIRST GYPSY: A cuckold?

SGANARELLE: Yes! Will I become a *cuckold?*

BOTH GYPSIES: [*banging their tambourines and singing*] La, la, la, la, la, la, la—

SGANARELLE: That's no answer. Come now, I've asked you both if I'll be a cuckold?

SECOND GYPSY: What, you, a cuckold?

SGANARELLE: Yes, will I?

FIRST GYPSY: A cuckold, you?

SGANARELLE: *Yes!* Will I or won't I?

BOTH GYPSIES: [*singing again*] La, la, la, la, la, la, la, la—

SGANARELLE: A pox on you both, you sluts, for leaving me stuck on the horns of my dilemma!

> [*The* GYPSIES *go off, slowly, still singing and playing their tambourines.*]

I must know how my marriage is going to turn out. Perhaps I can find that wise old magician everybody calls the king of the crystal ball. He grants all your wishes. Wait; perhaps I don't need a magician. The answer may be coming toward me.

> [*He hides behind the corner of his house.*]

> [DORIMÈNE *enters with* LYCASTE, *a young man.*]

LYCASTE: My lovely Dorimène, are you joking?

DORIMÈNE: I'm not joking.

LYCASTE: You're getting married in a short while?

DORIMÈNE: A very short while.

LYCASTE: And the wedding takes place——

DORIMÈNE: This evening.

LYCASTE: Can you be cruel enough to forget my love and wipe out the promises you gave me?

DORIMÈNE: Certainly not. I look on you with as much affection as ever. Don't let this marriage upset you. I'm not marrying the man for love; he's very rich, while I have nothing. And neither have you. Without money a girl can't advance far in society, so I must get it however I can. This is my opportunity to make an easy life for myself. I expect to be rid of the old codger before long; I doubt if he has more than six months left in him. Once we're married I'll pray every night to become a widow.

> [SGANARELLE, *who has not been able to see or hear properly, edges toward the others.* DORIMÈNE *spots him. He starts.*]

DORIMÈNE: Well, there you are. We were just speaking about you with the respect you deserve.

LYCASTE: Is this the gentleman who——

DORIMÈNE: Yes, this is the gentleman who is taking me as his wife.

LYCASTE: Allow me, Monsieur, to compliment you on your marriage, and to put myself humbly at your service. I can assure you that you are marrying a wonderful woman. And I rejoice with you, Mademoiselle Dorimène, in the happy choice you have made. You could not have done better; Monsieur has the air of a fine, strong husband. Yes, Monsieur, I hope to be your friend—to increase our friendship and deepen it by visiting you from time to time for a little business and some entertainment.

DORIMÈNE: [*to* LYCASTE] You do us both too much honor. But I must hurry away to prepare for the wedding. Later we'll have all the leisure we need to meet and enjoy ourselves.

> [*She goes out.* LYCASTE *bows too formally and too many times to both of them and goes off in the other direction.*]

SGANARELLE: Now I'm sure. I'm completely off marriage. The wisest thing I can do is to try to get out of it while there's still time. The engagement has already cost me enough, but it's better to overlook a few expenses than to get involved in a lot more. Let me see if I can wriggle out of this trap.

> [*He knocks on the door of the house that adjoins his.* ALCANTOR *opens up.*]

ALCANTOR: Son-in-law! Welcome.

SGANARELLE: At your service, Monsieur.

ALCANTOR: Have you come for the wedding?

SGANARELLE: I'm sorry to bother you.

ALCANTOR: No bother. I'm as impatient as I can see you are.

SGANARELLE: I've come, actually, about something else.

ALCANTOR: Don't fret yourself; everything is prepared for the reception.

SGANARELLE: It's nothing to do with that.

ALCANTOR: [*tugging him inside*] The orchestra is hired, the food has been ordered, and my daughter is ready to greet you.

SGANARELLE: [*resisting*] That's not why I came.

ALCANTOR: [*tugging again*] It will all be done to your satisfaction.

SGANARELLE: [*trying to break free*] But I have something to explain.

ALCANTOR: [*pulling violently*] Come in, my dear son-in-law, come in.

SGANARELLE: [*digging in his heels*] One word first.

ALCANTOR: [*dragging at* SGANARELLE *with both hands*] Let's not be formal. Come along inside, please.

SGANARELLE: [*breaking away and leaving a sleeve with* ALCANTOR] Not yet. First, I have a statement to make.

ALCANTOR: Oh, a statement?

SGANARELLE: YES!

ALCANTOR: Then make it.

SGANARELLE: Alcantor, I asked for your daughter's hand, and you kindly consented. But now I think things over, I realize that I may be a few years older than she is, and not quite suitable for her.

ALCANTOR: Pardon me, but my daughter is perfectly happy with you the way you are, and I am sure she will continue to be.

SGANARELLE: [*retreating from* ALCANTOR'S *reaching arms*] She doesn't know me. I have the strangest personal habits. And she'll never be able to put up with my temper.

ALCANTOR: [*advancing*] She's an easygoing girl. She'll get used to you.

SGANARELLE: [*retreating*] I have a few minor physical deformities and deficiencies that may disgust her.

ALCANTOR: [*following*] Nothing at all. An honest wife never feels disgust for her husband.

SGANARELLE: [*kneeling*] What else can I say? I advise you, I beg of you, not to give her to me.

ALCANTOR: [*stopping in shock*] Are you serious? I would die rather than go back on my word.

SGANARELLE: Please, I'll pay you for everything.

ALCANTOR: Never! I promised her to you, and you shall have her, no matter how many other men are clamoring for her.

SGANARELLE: How can I put it more plainly?

ALCANTOR: [*advancing again*] You see, I have a very special affection for you. I would turn down a prince so that you could have my daughter.

SGANARELLE: [*shouting*] Alcantor, thank you for the honor. The fact is I do not want to get married at all.

ALCANTOR: Oh, you do not?

SGANARELLE: I do not.

ALCANTOR: And why not, pray?

SGANARELLE: Because I don't feel ready for marriage. And also because I want to be like my father and his forefathers before him; none of them wanted to get married.

ALCANTOR: You are entitled to do what you want. I am not the man to constrain anybody. You arranged with me to marry my daughter and everything is now ready for it, except you. You want to retract your word. But never mind. I'll see what can be done. You will hear from me very soon.

[*He goes inside.*]

SGANARELLE: Well, he's more reasonable than I expected. I was sure it would be harder than this to break off. The more I think about it, the better I feel at having pulled out in time. I would have spent many years repenting. Who's this? The son? Is he bringing the reply?

[ALCIDAS, *the son of* ALCANTOR, *comes through the door. He is dressed in a swordsman's outfit and carries two épées.*]

ALCIDAS: [*with exaggerated civility*] Monsieur, I am very humbly at your service.

SGANARELLE: Even more humbly at yours.

ALCIDAS: My father tells me, Monsieur, that you have come to break your obligation?

SGANARELLE: I regret it, Monsieur, but yes.

ALCIDAS: But, Monsieur, there is nothing wrong in that.

SGANARELLE: I am most upset, I assure you. I'd hoped that——

ALCIDAS: I repeat; it's nothing.

[*He draws one of the swords swiftly, flexes it, swishes it in the air, bends his knees, cuts, parries, thrusts, and then holds out the two swords.*]

Would you be kind enough to choose?

SGANARELLE: One of these swords?

ALCIDAS: If you please.

SGANARELLE: For what?

ALCIDAS: Monsieur, you refuse to marry my sister after giving your word. I am sure you will not take offense at the compliment I have just offered you.

SGANARELLE: At the what?

ALCIDAS: Other families would make a fuss, but we believe in being gentle and gentlemanly. I therefore propose, in all courtesy, that we attempt to slit each other's throats.

SGANARELLE: As a compliment, it's unusual.

ALCIDAS: Let us now proceed, Monsieur. Please make your choice.

SGANARELLE: At your generous service, Monsieur, but I don't wish to cut anybody's throat. [*aside*] This polite talk scares the hell out of me.

ALCIDAS: There is no other way. Now, Monsieur, if you don't mind——

SGANARELLE: I do mind. [*weeping*] I don't want to.

ALCIDAS: You refuse to fight?

SGANARELLE: Oh, God, yes.

ALCIDAS: Is that your last word?

SGANARELLE: It is, it is—

ALCIDAS: In that case, Monsieur, you have no cause for complaint. I have done my best to behave properly in the circumstances. You have gone back on your word, and you decline my invitation to fight. Therefore [*He produces a short stick.*] I am compelled to strike you a few blows with this stick, according to the rules of etiquette. I know that you are too much of a gentleman to disapprove of my actions.

SGANARELLE: [*aside*] The man's a fiend.

ALCIDAS: Now, Monsieur, shall we begin? You would not want me to do this by force?

SGANARELLE: By f-f-force?

ALCIDAS: Monsieur, I never compel an opponent to do anything against his wishes. You must volunteer either to take a beating or to marry my sister.

SGANARELLE: I don't want to volunteer for either one.

ALCIDAS: Are you sure?

SGANARELLE: Quite sure.

ALCIDAS: I am stricken with remorse, Monsieur, to have to treat you in this fashion, but I have no decent alternative.

> [*He pursues* SGANARELLE *about the stage and administers a blow of the stick with each word that follows.*]

I will not let up unless you promise to fight me or to marry my sister.

SGANARELLE: [*crying out after each blow*] All right. I give in. I'll marry her! I'll marry her!

ALCIDAS: [*shaking his hand*] I am delighted that you understand my point of view and that matters can be settled amicably. [*dusting him down*] After all, I admire you more than any other man I know, and I would have felt very badly if you had compelled me to mistreat you. Now, with your permission, I shall call my father and tell him that we have reached an agreement.

> [*He goes inside.* SGANARELLE *collapses.*]

> [ALCIDAS *reappears, with* ALCANTOR.]

So you see, Father, Monsieur is perfectly reasonable and compliant. He wants to behave fairly, and you may now present him with my sister.

ALCANTOR: Sganarelle, here is my daughter's hand.

> [*He reaches into the doorway for* DORIMÈNE'*s hand. She appears shyly and goes to* SGANARELLE, *who gets painfully to his feet.*]

Praise be to heaven! I'm rid of her at last, and from now on you are responsible for her. Let us all celebrate this happy, happy union!

> [*Music, dance, and the wedding between a resigned* SGANARELLE *and a joyful* DORIMÈNE, *who goes to dance, as soon as the ceremony is over, with* LYCASTE.]

CURTAIN

The Seductive Countess

Molière concerned himself in several plays with provincial pretenders. The two *précieuses ridicules* Cathos and Magdelon have just arrived in Paris from the country; George Dandin's in-laws give themselves airs because they regard themselves as people "of quality"; Pourceaugnac is a self-styled "gentleman from Limoges who has studied law." La Comtesse d'Escarbagnas is Pourceaugnac's feminine counterpart, richly unaware of the indignity of her presence and as convinced of her virtues and attractions as is the Marquess Acaste in *The Misanthrope*. Molière is said to have taken her character from life; there was, it seems, a lady from Angoulême named Sarah de Pérusse, whose father was the Comte d'*Escars* and whose husband was the Comte de *Baignac*. By eliding the two names Molière found the lady a title and the play caused great mirth when it was staged in Angoulême, whose inhabitants remembered the by-then-dead original. The text as it has come down to us is far from complete. It was performed in December, 1671, in honor of the second marriage of Louis XIV's brother, Philippe d'Orléans, and contained a sumptuous spectacle (the text of which has been lost), incorporating ballet and Lully's music; the overall title of the show was "The Ballet of Ballets." The beginning of *The Seductive Countess* led into the spectacular business, which was the show supposedly written by the Vicomte in the play for the Comtesse. The spectacle was then interrupted by the arrival of Monsieur Harpin (on whom Lesage may later have based his businessman in *Turcaret*) with his blue language; the play closed with the final (and feeble) unknotting of the plot. The plot itself hardly exists; the play is a hook on which to dangle the Comtesse, in more ways than one, and after her first entrance the story as such hardly matters. When the play was moved from Saint-Germain-en-Laye to Paris, to run in harness with *The Forced Marriage,* the original "ballet of ballets" spectacle was dropped and new music interpolated by Charpentier; Molière had been involved in a serious quarrel with Lully over the management of the Palais-Royal. The audiences in Paris took to the play immediately. The version given here is very lightly modified toward the end so as to make it self-contained in English.

THE SEDUCTIVE COUNTESS

La Comtesse d'Escarbagnas

―――

CHARACTERS:

THE COMTESSE D'ESCARBAGNAS
THE VICOMTE, in love with Julie
JULIE, a protégée of the Comtesse, in love with the Vicomte
MONSIEUR TIBAUDIER, councillor, an admirer of the Comtesse
MONSIEUR HARPIN, tax-collector, another suitor to the Comtesse
THE COMTE, young son of the Comtesse
MONSIEUR BOBINET, tutor to the Comte
ANDRÉE, chambermaid to the Comtesse
JEANNOT, pageboy to Tibaudier
CRIQUET, pageboy to the Comtesse

Scene: Angoulême.

―――

[*The drawing room of the* COMTESSE's *house in Angoulême, a small city about seventy miles northeast of Bordeaux. The* COMTESSE *is a comfortably left widow, and the room is furnished to bulging point with heavily up-holstered furniture, knickknacks and bric-a-brac on every flat surface, and idealized portraits of the* COMTESSE *and the late* COMTE. JULIE, *a pretty girl of about twenty, is waiting—has been waiting for about half an hour—for the* VICOMTE. *She is almost ready to give him up when he enters.*]

VICOMTE: What's this, Julie? You're already here?

JULIE: Yes, you should be ashamed of yourself, Cléante. It's hardly polite for a young man to arrive after his sweetheart.

VICOMTE: I would have been here an hour ago, but it was just my luck to run into an old fellow I know, one of those self-styled

147

men of quality. He insisted on asking me what news I had of the Court; that was his excuse to launch into all the extravagant stories he's picked up himself lately. One of the curses of life in a small town is the rumor-monger who is always looking for someone on whom he can empty out all the slops he's gathered. This one started by showing me two newspaper sheets crammed to the margins with piffle and tattle which come, says he, from an absolutely reliable source. He then proceeds—making a great mystery out of it—to read me the recent misinformation from *The Dutch Gazette,* which bored me to distraction,[1] followed by the decrees and instructions issued by our Ministry of Defense, from which I thought he'd never emerge. To hear him talk you'd say he keeps the members of the Cabinet abreast of what's going on in this country. He's in on every state secret; nobody makes a move without consulting him. He expounds the hidden, under-lying reasons for our policies—to say nothing of the policies of neighboring countries. In his own mind he conducts the affairs of Europe. And not only of Europe. His private intelligence services operate as far afield as Africa and Asia; he watches the activities of Prester John in Abyssinia[2] and the Grand Mogol of Mongolia.

JULIE: You're spinning out your excuse as skillfully as you can to make it interesting and to make me forgive you.

VICOMTE: Honestly, my sweet Julie, that's the true reason why I was late. If I wanted to offer the conventional polite excuses I would merely say that I was reluctant to come to an appointment with the Comtesse, kind though you were to arrange it for me; that I didn't want to be the first one here for fear of having to pay court to her; that I forced myself to come only to please you; that I am embarrassed to meet her except when you're present to get some entertainment out of it; that I detest these little chats with the stupid woman; and that, finally, since I come here only to see you, I wanted to delay my arrival until I knew you would be here.

---

[1] *The Dutch Gazette (La Gazette de Hollande)* was eagerly scanned by French readers for clues to political maneuvers between Holland and France.

[2] Prester John was a fictitious character, a Westerner and a Christian who was thought to govern an empire in Asia. In the fifteenth century he was somehow mentally transported (under the name Prêtre-Jean or Prête-Jean) by the French to Abyssinia, where he survived until the end of the seventeenth century.

JULIE: I realize that you aren't lacking in ingenuity and that you know how to paint your faults in appealing colors. Still, if you'd come half an hour earlier we could have profited from the extra time together, because when I arrived the Comtesse had already gone out. I suspect that she's now parading through the town and spreading the word about the play you wrote for me and pretended to dedicate to her.

VICOMTE: But when are you going to put an end to these awkward sessions here and let me see you privately?

JULIE: When our parents consent to it, and I've no idea when that will be. You know as well as I do that, with this quarrel between our families, we can't meet anywhere else. My brothers, not to mention your father, won't tolerate a match between us.

VICOMTE: But why not make the most of our meetings if they must be held in secret? I see no reason for this tedious business of pretending to be a suitor to the old hag.

JULIE: It's the best way to conceal our love. Besides, to tell you the truth, I do love watching you play up to her. I doubt whether your new comedy will make me laugh more. She really is a theatrical figure, you know, with her talk about being a lady of quality. Her trip to Paris, her introduction to Court circles, and her attempt to bring fine manners back with her to Angoulême are giving her performance that final polish. Every day she's been adding delightful new touches.

VICOMTE: Yes, but you don't stop to think that your game is torture for me. I can't keep it up; I'm too seriously in love with you. It's cruel to let this frolic take up so much of the time that I would rather spend on telling you how much I love you. Last night I wrote a few lines on this very theme, and I can't stop myself from saying them to you—unless you tell me not to. That's the poet's vice: he yearns to recite his verse.

> You hold me, Iris, at the stake too long.

By Iris, of course, I mean Julie.

> You hold me, Iris, at the stake too long.
> I may obey your laws, but I deplore
> The tactics you impose. Ah, you are wrong
> To make me kneel to someone I abhor.

Why must those lovely eyes, which I adore,
Turn away from my sighs? I cannot measure
How I have suffered from your charms, and more,
How I now suffer further for your pleasure.

And thus I face two martyrdoms at once:
I must speak out, yet I must bear the brunts
Of love in silence, swallowing my pain.

You light a flame and then you let it wane.
Try to be merciful, in heaven's name,
Or I must end my life to end this game.

JULIE: You make yourself out to be much worse treated than you really are. That, I suppose, is poetic license: talking about martyrdoms and pretending your mistress is cruel, before she has a chance to complain about you. All the same, I hope you'll give me the poem in writing.

VICOMTE: I've spoken it; that was all I wanted to do. Sometimes one may be foolish enough to compose a poem; one should never be foolish enough to let it be read.

JULIE: There's no need for false modesty. People know that you have a literary gift. Why should you hide it?

VICOMTE: Please, we'll go no further with this until I have something better to show you. It's dangerous to have literary gifts in this society. You expose yourself to ridicule; some of our friends have already set me an example.

JULIE: Cléante, you are wasting your breath. I can see clearly that you're dying to give me a copy of that poem, and you'll be most disappointed if I don't press you for it.

VICOMTE: You're making fun of me. I'm not as much of a poet as you might think— But here comes the venerable Comtesse d'Escarbagnas. I'll leave by the other door to avoid her, and start preparing the entertainment I promised you.

> [*He goes out by a side door. Through the main doorway comes the* COMTESSE, *with an uncertain pageboy,* CRIQUET, *dawdling behind her.*]

COMTESSE: Madame, you are alone? What a dreadful pity! All alone! I thought my servants said that the Vicomte was here?

JULIE: He did come, but as soon as he saw you were not about, he left.

COMTESSE: But he did see you?

JULIE: Yes.

COMTESSE: Didn't he say anything?

JULIE: No, Madame. That must mean that he is completely yours.

COMTESSE: Really, that wasn't nice. I shall have to tell him off. However desperately he desires me, I wouldn't like to think that my suitors neglect their duty to the rest of my sex. I am definitely not one of those selfish women who enjoy watching their admirers snub other damsels.

JULIE: You mustn't be surprised at what he did, Madame. His love for you lights up every word he says and every move he makes. He has eyes for nobody else.

COMTESSE: I realize that I am capable of inspiring a powerful passion in men; you must blame that on my beauty, my youth and my quality, for all of which I thank heaven. Nevertheless, even the man who is drunk and blind in his devotion should remember to be civil toward others. Lackey, what are you doing there? Can't you wait in an antechamber until you are called? It's so perplexing; in the provinces you simply cannot find a lackey who knows his manners. Yes, I'm talking to you, scamp. Outside with you. Now, where are my ladies?

[CRIQUET *goes out.*]

[ANDRÉE, *the chambermaid, comes in, dressed in cleaning clothes.*]

ANDRÉE: You called, Madame?

COMTESSE: Remove my coifs. Gently now, with your great peasant's hands. You'll shake my head off.

ANDRÉE: Sorry, Madame. I'm doing it as gentle as I can.

COMTESSE: Yes, but your gentleness is too rough for my head. There—now you've dislocated my neck. Take my muff. Hold it up; don't let it hang like that. And put it away in my cloakroom. Where is she going? Where *is* she going? What is the little goose up to?

ANDRÉE: I was just taking your muff and your coifs down to the cellar. You did say the coke-room?

COMTESSE: The impudence of her! [*to* JULIE] Excuse this disgusting exhibition. [*to* ANDRÉE] Now listen to me, animal, I said cloakroom, the place where I keep my clothes.

ANDRÉE: Oh, the wardrobe. Is that what they call it in Paris, the coke-room?

COMTESSE: Yes, dimwit, the cloakroom is where you hang your garments.

ANDRÉE: I won't forget that, Madame. And I'll remember to call your attic the junkroom.

[*She goes out.*]

COMTESSE: How difficult it is to teach a little delicacy to these wild beasts.

JULIE: I think they're very happy to be under your instruction.

COMTESSE: That girl is the daughter of my old nurse. She is still new at this sort of thing. I took her on as a chambermaid.

JULIE: That is the act of a good heart, Madame. It is noble to make oneself responsible for these poor souls.

COMTESSE: [*shouting*] Chairs, we need chairs! Lackeys, where are you all? It's positively humiliating not to have a lackey to set up the chairs. Ladies! Lackeys! Lackeys! Ladies! Somebody! Anybody! I think all my servants must be dead and we shall have to take our own chairs.

[ANDRÉE *reenters.*]

ANDRÉE: Yes, Madame?

COMTESSE: Must I wear out my throat on you people?

ANDRÉE: I was putting away your muff and coifs in the ward—in the coke-room.

COMTESSE: Call that pup of a lackey for me.

ANDRÉE: Hey! Criquet!

COMTESSE: That's enough of the yodeling. What do you think you are? A goat girl? He's not Criquet. He's the lackey.

ANDRÉE: Lackey, then, not Criquet, Madame wants you. Criq— Lack— *Crackey!*

[CRIQUET *comes in slowly.*]

CRIQUET: What is it?

COMTESSE: Where have you been, worm?

CRIQUET: Out in the street, Madame.

COMTESSE: Why, pray, in the street?

CRIQUET: You said to go outside.

COMTESSE: You're a young sluggard and it's time that you learned that when a lady of quality says "outside" she means in her antechamber. Andrée, be sure to borrow a whip from my equerry and give this blockhead a thorough thrashing.

ANDRÉE: Who's your querry, Madame? D'you mean Charles the gardener?

COMTESSE: Silence, slut. The instant you open your mouth some impertinence flies out of it. Chairs—here—now! And you, insect, go and light two expensive wax candles in my silver chandelier. It's getting late. Why are you looking at me like a madwoman?

ANDRÉE: We—I—there is no expensive wax candles, Madame. They're all cheap tallow.

COMTESSE: Oh, you spider! What happened to the expensive wax I ordered a few days ago?

ANDRÉE: I haven't seen none in the house since I've been here.

COMTESSE: Get out of my sight. I can see I'll have to send you back to your parents. Bring me a glass of water.

> [ANDRÉE *goes out tearfully. Now begins the ceremony of the chairs.*]

Pray take this one, Madame.

JULIE: Only if you don't wish to take it, Madame.

COMTESSE: I don't, Madame.

JULIE: Then I will, Madame.

COMTESSE: Then I will take this one, Madame.

JULIE: Pray do, Madame.

COMTESSE: Thank you, Madame.

JULIE: Thank *you*, Madame.

COMTESSE: Comfortable, Madame?

JULIE: Eminently, Madame.

COMTESSE: Be frank with me, Madame, now that we are informal and at ease in my own little dwelling. Would you say I was provincial?

JULIE: Heaven forbid, Madame.

[ANDRÉE *comes in with the glass of water.*]

COMTESSE: What's this? Where is my saucer? You know that I never touch water without a saucer.

ANDRÉE: [*to* CRIQUET, *who is looking on*] What's a saucer?

CRIQUET: A what?

ANDRÉE: Yes.

CRIQUET: Never heard of it.

COMTESSE: Are you giving me the lie?

ANDRÉE: Honest, Madame, we don't know what a what-you-said is.

COMTESSE: [*with exaggerated patience*] Learn then, my child, that a saucer is a plate upon which one rests the glass. Ah, Paris is the place for service! You have no more to do than blink there and they understand.

[CRIQUET *hands a plate to* ANDRÉE. *She places it on top of the glass.*]

COMTESSE: Not there, you lump. How many times have I told you? The saucer goes underneath.

ANDRÉE: Soon fix that.

[*She drops the plate.*]

COMTESSE: Stars above, heavens, stars, moons! You'll pay for that saucer.

ANDRÉE: Very good, Madame.

COMTESSE: The vexing girl, the vixen, the clod, the witch——

ANDRÉE: Damn, it, Madame, if I pay for it I don't stand for no insults.

[*She marches out.*]

COMTESSE: Away, away, you pollute my eyes. It's so disconcerting, Madame, in these small towns. They simply do not know a *thing*. Whenever I return to the bucolic life I throw up my hands at the lack of respect for my quality.

JULIE: How could they know better? They've never been to Paris.

COMTESSE: They do not wish to learn. If they would only keep their ears open! What annoys me most is that they think they know as much as I do, even though I spent two whole months in Paris and met the entire Court.

JULIE: These are essentially narrow people.

COMTESSE: I can't bear their mania for treating everyone alike. After all, some people have to be inferior to others; it's in the nature of things. It incenses me to hear a local upstart with a new municipal title pretending to be as good as my late husband, a man who had his own hounds and horses, who lived in the country by choice, and who always signed his name *Comte* d'Escarbagnas.

JULIE: They know how to live in Paris. You must cherish the memory of the hotels.

COMTESSE: *Quite* distinct from what we have here, I can tell you. The cream of the aristocracy comes visiting and pays you every respect you could wish for. You don't have to move from your chair. And if you wish to see a revue or that ballet, *Psyché*,[3] the tickets are booked for you.

JULIE: I daresay, Madame, that you conquered many noble hearts.

COMTESSE: Heavens above, Madame, I swear there wasn't a gallant in the city who didn't come to see me and make pretty conversation. I still have all their notes in my purse, and they would give you some idea of the number of proposals I rejected. No need to tell you the names; when I say "all the gallants," you'll know the ones I mean, *all* of them.

JULIE: What surprises me, Madame, is that after receiving all those lofty names, which I hardly dare guess at, you are now reduced to a mere councillor, Monsieur Tibaudier, and a tax-collector, Monsieur Harpin. What a fall was there— But the Vicomte now: he is, at least, a nobleman, even though he is in the provinces, and he can always pay a trip to Paris if he feels so inclined. But a councillor and a tax-collector offer meager possibilities to so great a lady as yourself.

COMTESSE: But what choice does one have in these rural wilds? Those two do serve to fill the gaps where there are no gallants; they make up the numbers. It's advisable, Madame, not to let one suitor become sole master of one's terrain. Without rivals he becomes careless, indifferent, slothful.

JULIE: Madame, I assure you that I profit wondrously from every-

---

[3] Written earlier the same year by Molière, Corneille, and Quinault, *Psyché* was a "tragedy-cum-ballet" with music by Lully; it had been commissioned to open the new theater in the Tuileries.

thing you say. Your conversation is a college where I learn something new each day.

[CRIQUET *and* ANDRÉE *come in with* JEANNOT.]

CRIQUET: Jeannot's here to see you. The councillor sent him.

COMTESSE: Ape! Barbarian! Don't you know how to announce a visitor? You whisper to my lady-in-waiting, and she comes over to me and says quietly, "Madame, a lackey has arrived from Monsieur Tibaudier the councillor, and requests a word with you." To which I reply, "Bid him enter."

CRIQUET: Over here, Jeannot.

COMTESSE: Another mistake. What is it, lackey? What do you bring there?

JEANNOT: Monsieur Tibaudier sends you the greetings of the day, Madame, and before he makes an appearance would like to offer you these pears[4] from his garden, with this note attached.

COMTESSE: Oh, how charming! They're Good-Christians, the finest pears grown. Andrée, take them to the cook and ask her to wrap them carefully and put them away in the food conserver. There, my boy, buy yourself a lemonade.

JEANNOT: No, thank you, Madame.

COMTESSE: I say yes.

JEANNOT: My master told me not to take a tip from you.

COMTESSE: Never mind that.

JEANNOT: Forgive me, Madame.

CRIQUET: What's up with you, Jeannot? Take it. If you don't want it pass it on to me.

[JEANNOT *takes the tip.*]

COMTESSE: Tell your master that I thank him for his pears.

CRIQUET: [*going out with* JEANNOT] All right, hand it over.

JEANNOT: Yes, like a loony I will.

CRIQUET: But I told you to take it.

---

[4] Just as the French word for a horn (*corne*) always raises a guffaw from a French audience because of its intimations of cuckoldry, so the words for pear and pears (*poire, poires*) suggest infidelity or mischief.

JEANNOT: I was going to take it anyway.

[*They go out, wrestling for the coin.*]

COMTESSE: What I like about Monsieur Tibaudier is that he knows how to pay his respects to a woman of my quality.

[CRIQUET *comes back with the* VICOMTE.]

CRIQUET: In there.

[*The* COMTESSE *winces.*]

VICOMTE: Madame, I have come to let you know that the play will be ready shortly; we can go to the theater in fifteen minutes.

COMTESSE: I don't want any rabble there. Tell my footman not to let any of the scum in.

VICOMTE: In that case, Madame, I must inform you that I will have to bow out. The performance will give me no pleasure if there are not enough spectators. Take my word, you'll enjoy it much more if you have a large audience from all over the town.

COMTESSE: Lackey, a chair for the Vicomte. You have come just in time to do me a tiny favor. Here is a note I received from Monsieur Tibaudier, together with some Good-Christian pears. I haven't looked at it yet. Would you please read it to me?

VICOMTE: [*skimming the note*] Well, well, this is written in fine style and deserves to be read aloud:

"Madame, I could never tender you this gift did I not harvest more fruit from my garden than I pluck from my love——"

COMTESSE: That shows clearly that there is nothing whatsoever between us.

VICOMTE: [*continuing*] "The pears have not yet ripened, but they match the hardness of your soul, which, after the constant rebuffs I have suffered, promises me no pearlike sweetness. Yet, Madame, I ask you to believe that if I were to enumerate your perfections, eternity would not suffice for the recital of my list. I conclude these brief words with a plea that you account me as much of a good Christian as these pears I dispatch to you, since I am rendering good for evil; or, to speak plainly, I am presenting you with these Good-Christian pears in exchange for the sour, stony pears of cruelty, which you compel me to swallow daily. I remain your unworthy slave, *Tibaudier.*"

That, Madame, is a letter to keep.

COMTESSE: I detected one or two words that the Academy would frown upon;[5] but I like the respect he shows for me.

JULIE: You're correct, Madame. Without wishing to offend Monsieur le Vicomte, I must say that I could love a man who sent me such a letter.

[TIBAUDIER *appears nervously at the door.*]

COMTESSE: Approach our person, Monsieur Tibaudier. You need not fear to enter. Your letter was well received, as were your pears, and this young lady has just spoken up for you against your rival here.

TIBAUDIER: I am much obliged to her, Madame; if she is ever involved in a lawsuit in this municipality she shall see that I am not unmindful of the honor she does me in becoming the advocate of my passion in respect of your beauty.

JULIE: You need no advocate, Monsieur Tibaudier. Your cause is just.

TIBAUDIER: Nevertheless, Madame, the best cause must be persuasively presented. I have reason to apprehend seeing my affections supplanted by those of my rival and Madame swayed by the title of a Vicomte.

VICOMTE: I had some small hopes, Monsieur, before I saw your letter. Now, I confess, I am fearful for my love.

TIBAUDIER: Here, in addition, Madame, are two verselets that I have composed in your honor and to your glory.

VICOMTE: Ah, I had no idea that Monsieur Tibaudier was a poet too. Those verselets will wreck my chances for good and all.

COMTESSE: He means strophes, not verselets.[6] Lackey, find a chair for Monsieur Tibaudier. With a soft back, baboon. Now, Monsieur, make yourself comfortable and read us your strophes.

TIBAUDIER: A lady of quality
    Drives my love mad.
    In spite of her jollity
    I'm very sad.

---

[5] The French Academy had been founded thirty-six years earlier (in 1635) by Richelieu, and its influence had grown directly and indirectly since. Nonacademic authors like Molière have always poked fun at it.

[6] The Comtesse is here correcting one error with another.

Why does she add
Scorn to frivolity?

VICOMTE: After that, I'm lost.

COMTESSE: The first line is superb: "A lady of quality."

JULIE: It's rather lengthy, but one must take risks when expressing a picturesque thought.

COMTESSE: And now, please, the second strophe.

TIBAUDIER: I know not if you doubt my love one drop.
I do, however, know that this, my heart,
Would if it could walk out of its apart-
Ment and pay court to yours, Madame, nonstop.
Then afterwards you'd see my tenderness
Was even more than you had guessed, not less.
Henceforward you would say
That you were satisfied to be a Comtesse:
You'd strip away that skin of a tig*ress*
Which you wear night and day.

VICOMTE: I'm undone. Tibaudier has undone me.

COMTESSE: Don't make fun. For a country poem, it's not at all bad.

VICOMTE: Make fun, I? Although I am his opponent, I consider his poem remarkable. I would not talk of strophes, as you did. Rather, I would call them elegies or metamorphoses, and worth any written by Ovid.[7]

COMTESSE: Whom? Ovid? Does he write poems? I thought he sold gloves.

TIBAUDIER: This is a different Ovid, Madame, an author who died thirty or forty years ago.

VICOMTE: It is obvious that Monsieur Tibaudier has read his poets. Now let us see whether my music, comedy, and ballet can compete with his letter and strophes.

COMTESSE: I am waiting for my son the Comte to join us. He came back from my chateau this morning with his tutor. Ah, I think I see the tutor waiting in the antechamber.

---

[7] In the French text, the Vicomte talks not of Ovid's works but of Martial's epigrams. The Comtesse mistakes the name for that of a Martial who was a fashionable glovemaker and perfumer in Paris. The name of Ovid has been substituted because he may be more familiar to English-speaking audiences, and also because Martial sounds more like Marshall.

[MONSIEUR BOBINET, *the tutor, pushes his head in.*]

COMTESSE: Good day, Monsieur Bobinet. Come in, Monsieur Bobinet. Let me introduce you to society.

BOBINET: [*coming forward*] I wish the honorable company good eventide. What do you wish of your loyal servant, Madame?

COMTESSE: At what time did you leave my estate at Escarbagnas with my son the Comte?

BOBINET: At eight forty-five, Madame, as you desired us to do.

COMTESSE: How were my other two sons, the Marquess and the Commander?

BOBINET: In glowing health, Madame, heaven be praised.

COMTESSE: Where is the Comte?

BOBINET: In your sumptuous alcove outside.

COMTESSE: What is he doing?

BOBINET: Writing a composition I set, Madame, on an epistle of Cicero.

COMTESSE: Bring him in, Monsieur Bobinet.

BOBINET: With all my heart, Madame.

[*He goes out.*]

VICOMTE: This Monsieur Bobinet has a wise face, Madame, and I think he's not without wit.

[MONSIEUR BOBINET *returns with the young* COMTE.]

BOBINET: Now, Monsieur le Comte, let us show this dignified gathering how you have profited from your studies. First a sweeping bow to the entire room.

COMTESSE: Now a separate bow for Madame. A gesture of reverence for Monsieur le Vicomte. And another for Monsieur Tibaudier.

TIBAUDIER: I am ravished, Madame, at the honor you do me. May I embrace the young gentleman? Thank you. One cannot love the trunk and not the branches.

COMTESSE: Monsieur Tibaudier, I am not sure that I like that metaphor.

JULIE: He makes a most impressive impression.

VICOMTE: He is striding forward manfully to take his place in society.

JULIE: Who would believe that Madame had so grown-up a child?

COMTESSE: I was terribly young when I bore him, still playing with dolls.

JULIE: He looks more like your brother.

COMTESSE: Take good care of his education, Monsieur Bobinet.

BOBINET: Madame, I neglect nothing in my cultivation of this young plant. I am honored that you have entrusted his upbringing to me, and I shall endeavor to inculcate in him the seeds of virtue.

COMTESSE: Let's hear something you've taught him. Make him say something clever.

BOBINET: With pleasure. Young man, recite the lesson I taught you yesterday.

COMTE: "Let every name that is apt only for a man be masculine. Let——"

COMTESSE: Stop! Monsieur Bobinet, what's all this foolishness you're teaching him?

BOBINET: From the Latin, Madame, the first rule of one of our great scholars.[8]

COMTESSE: I don't like this scholar or his work. In future I hope you'll teach Latin that's a little easier to understand.

BOBINET: If you allow the young gentleman to finish he can give you a glossary of the difficult words, to clarify the meaning.

COMTESSE: Clarifications are *not* necessary.

[CRIQUET *enters.*]

CRIQUET: The actors say they're ready.

COMTESSE: Then let us take our places. Monsieur Tibaudier, will you escort Madame?

[*They turn their chairs toward the auditorium, which represents the stage, and arrange them in rows. A few other spectators file in at the rear. The introductory notes are sounded by the violins, and the spectators sit back in expectation, all except* TIBAUDIER, *who seats himself on the floor at the feet of the* COMTESSE.]

---

[8] The scholar in question was the Flemish Jean Depautère, the author of a "Latin Grammar," a popular textbook of the seventeenth and eighteenth centuries.

VICOMTE: I should explain that the text of the play was written only to tie together the other elements: the music, the dance, and———

COMTESSE: Good grief, let's see it for ourselves. We have enough brains, I think, to understand it.

[MONSIEUR HARPIN *enters.*]

HARPIN: Well, I'll be a blue jay. This is a fine blue thing I see going on here.

COMTESSE: Monsieur Harpin, please! Coming in here like this with your blue language and interrupting our play!

HARPIN: Blue death, Madame, I'm bowled over by this business. At last I can see for my true-blue self how honest you were with your talk about being faithful.

COMTESSE: For mercy's sake, Monsieur, it's not done—to walk in so noisily when a performance is about to begin!

HARPIN: If you ask me, the real performance is the one you're giving, and if I'm interrupting that I don't give a blue damn.

[MONSIEUR BOBINET, *outraged, takes the young* COMTE *out of the room.*]

COMTESSE: Hush, you don't know what you're saying.

HARPIN: Don't I, by blue! I know all too blue well.

COMTESSE: Fie, fie, Monsieur, it's evil to swear in this fashion.

HARPIN: Buckets of blue, if there's anything evil going on, it's not my fault or my swearing but what's doing here with you. I'd rather see you letting your tongue loose on a few blue oaths than blueballing around with him.

VICOMTE: I don't think I understand what you're complaining about, Monsieur.

HARPIN: Now lookit, Vicomte, I don't want to squabble with you, and I'm blued if I blame you for pressing your attentions on her, and I'm sorry if I'm butting in on your show. But don't you blame me either, see? We both have bundles of blue reasons why we do what we're doing.

VICOMTE: I have nothing to say to you and I am puzzled at the nature of your mouthings at the Comtesse.

COMTESSE: When a gentleman is jealous he does not behave in this way, but rather brings his misgivings quietly to the ear of his beloved.

HARPIN: Quietly? Who, me?

COMTESSE: Yes, Monsieur, you. The theater is not the place where one goes trumpeting one's private grievances.

HARPIN: When it comes to *my* grievances, I open my blue mouth wherever I'm standing, and if I'm standing in a theater, then let the whole blue public hear what I have to say about you.

COMTESSE: Are you making all this fuss simply because the Vicomte has written a little comedy for me? Monsieur Tibaudier, another rival of the Vicomte, also loves me, but see how respectfully he uses me.

[TIBAUDIER *shows his head fearfully.*]

HARPIN: Tibaudier can use you however he likes. I don't know exactly what Tibaudier has been up to with you, but he's no example for me. You wouldn't catch me paying for a gang of blue-gutted violins so that other people can dance.

COMTESSE: Come now, Monsieur, you do not know what you are saying. You have no right to talk this way to a lady of quality. These people will think that there is some strange relationship between you and me.

HARPIN: Come off it. Cut out the guff.

COMTESSE: I fear that I don't understand what you mean by *guff*.

HARPIN: I mean I don't give a blue hoot if you fancy the Vicomte; you wouldn't be the first woman who plays about with these high-society blue-knows-whos, and was being chased by a tax-collector and betrayed his passion—*and* his purse—for the first johnny that takes her blue eyes. But don't expect me to be your blue dupe. I swear in front of all these people and by everything that's blue that I'm breaking off with you. From now on you'll collect nothing more from the tax-collector.

TIBAUDIER: [*getting to his feet*] Monsieur Harpin, we will meet at another place and I will demonstrate my prowess with points or pistols.

HARPIN: I'll be there, Tibaudier, and blue to you.

[*He goes out.*]

COMTESSE: I'm all confused by this impertinence.

VICOMTE: A jealous man, Madame, is like a plaintiff who has lost a case; he must be excused anything he says. Now, by blue—pardon me— Now let us pay attention to the play.

> [*They settle back to watch again, but* JEANNOT *enters with a note, which he gives to the* VICOMTE.]

JEANNOT: Monsieur, somebody asked me to hand you this note.

VICOMTE: [*reading*] "I am sending you advance notice of an incident that will be of interest to you. The dispute between your family and Julie's has been settled, on one condition: that you and she get married. Your friend, *Jacques*."

Well, well, Madame, that's the end of our comedy.

JULIE: Cléante, at last! [*They kiss.*] Who would have hoped for such a happy ending?

COMTESSE: What's all this? What are you talking about?

VICOMTE: Madame, I am about to marry Julie. And if you want to tie up all the loose ends in the play, you will marry Tibaudier and give Andrée to his lackey, who will thus become your footman.

COMTESSE: Alone! Deserted! Surrounded by traitors! Where can I turn?

TIBAUDIER: To me, dear lady. I have waited for nothing better.

COMTESSE: Yes, my darling Tibaudier, I will marry you if only to spite the others.

TIBAUDIER: The honor is mine.

VICOMTE: Madame, perhaps you will be good enough to contain your spite until the play is finished.

> [*Flourish of violins to announce the beginning of the play.*]

CURTAIN

Molière's Life and Works

A CHRONOLOGICAL SUMMARY

1622 — Born in January, exact date unknown, and christened on the 15th as Jean-Baptiste, first son of Jean and Marie Poquelin, who lived on the rue Saint-Honoré in Paris.

1632 — Mme Poquelin died, aged 31. About one year later Jean-Baptiste's father married Catherine Fleurette, who was also to die young (in 1636). The boy remained on close terms with his mother's father, Louis Cressé, who took him from time to time to see the Italian Players, renowned for their comedy, and the specialists in tragedy at the Hôtel de Bourgogne theater.

1633–39 — (These dates are uncertain.) Attended the Jesuit Collège de Clermont, a progressive high school for boys from wealthy and middling-to-wealthy families. His friends and fellows at Clermont included Cyrano de Bergerac, the poet Chapelle, and the young Prince de Conti. In 1637, his father, a furniture dealer and upholsterer, promised that his royal stipend, *tapissier ordinaire* to the King's household (the duties of which consisted mostly of supervising the royal bedchamber and making the royal bed), would be passed on to his son. Jean-Baptiste came to excel in classical studies, especially Latin. Although he was considered to be his father's successor in the upholstery business (retail and royal), he studied to become a lawyer. (1638 — birth of Louis XIV. 1639 — birth of Jean Racine.)

1641 — Received his law degree. Met and was smitten by Madeleine Béjart, a red-haired actress, playwright, and poet, four years his senior, and became friendly with her family: father, mother, and ten children, five of whom were stagestruck. Molière's father, upset by this affiliation, sent him on a trip with Louis XIII to Narbonne on the Mediterranean coast.

1642 — Took out his lawyer's papers at Orléans.

1643 — In January, he gave up his rights to the hereditary title ot *tapissier ordinaire* and in June, under the name of Molière, signed a contract with eleven other actors, among them Madeleine and her brother Joseph, incorporating a troupe called The Illustrious Theater. The troupe opened in Rouen in November while its theater in Paris was being built—Rouen was the home of Corneille, whose work was represented on the first season's playbill. (In February, Armande Béjart, Molière's wife-to-be, was born, whether to Madeleine—this would not have been her first illegitimate child—or to her mother Marie is not known.)

1644–45 — The Illustrious actors returned to Paris, mounted a run of tragedies, and whether through the severity of competition or their own lack of competence and experience or both, bankrupted themselves. In July and again in August, 1645, Molière was sentenced to the debtors' prison at Châtelet, but was released after one of his investors, Léonard Aubry, agreed to stand security. Aubry was subsequently repaid by Molière's father.

1646–50 — Paris seemed unresponsive to the young actors; so they moved out to the provinces under the direction of the actor-manager Dufresne and the patronage of the Duc d'Épernon, the governor of Guyenne province. They began to apply themselves to comedy and farce, interlarded with the tragedies of Corneille, du Ryer, and Rotrou. Madeleine was leading lady; Molière shared the leading male roles with two other actors. During these five years he wrote a number of small plays, of which two have come down to us, *La Jalousie du Barbouillé* (*The Jealous Husband*) and *Le Médecin volant* (*The Flying Doctor*). The troupe, with its complement of 20 to 25 performers, toured through many cities and small towns, mostly in the southwest and the Midi, including Nantes, Toulouse, Montpellier, and Narbonne. Among the actors was the celebrated René Berthelot or Gros-René or Monsieur du Parc, for whom Molière wrote several roles. (In 1653, Du Parc married a voluptuous carnival performer, Marquise-Thérèse de Gorla, with whom Pierre and Thomas Corneille, Racine, and numberless spectators were to fall in love.)

1650 — The company acquired a new patron, Armand de Bourbon, Prince de Conti, who had been at Clermont at the same time as

Molière; at this development Dufresne withdrew from managing the troupe, and Molière, as Conti's "favored actor," took his place. After 1653 Molière's productions radiated from Lyon to the surrounding towns, and enjoyed great popularity there; Lyon was a regular stopping place for the Italian troupes coming across the Alps into the south of France.

1653 or 1655 — Molière directed his first full-length comedy, *L'Étourdi* (*The Bungler*), written in verse and based on a play by Beltrame.

1656 — The Prince de Conti, hitherto a lover of women and theater, was suddenly converted to full-blooded Jansenism; he began to attack the theater in general and Molière in particular as immoral and antireligious. The company was now without a patron. Molière's second full-length play *Le Dépit amoureux* (*The Loving Quarrel*), also in verse, had its first performance in Béziers.

1658 — The company returned to Paris, still without a sponsor, stopping briefly at Rouen. In October after a fifteen-year absence they reopened in Paris in a room in the Louvre, before a royal audience. The King and his fellow spectators yawned during the uncoiling of Corneille's *Nicomedes,* but came awake during a short address given by Molière to introduce a little comedy he had played successfully outside Paris, *Le Médecin amoureux* (*The Doctor in Love*), the script of which has disappeared. Thenceforward, the King's brother, "Monsieur," gave the troupe his patronage, and its finances were assured. Molière was allowed to share the Petit-Bourbon theater with the Italian Players under Scaramouche, occupying the stage on Mondays, Wednesdays, Thursdays, and Saturdays. He moved into the Petit-Bourbon in November.

1659 — After finding that his comedies *The Bungler* and *The Reluctant Parting* were drawing more business than the tragedies, he wrote a new comedy in one act—it has been said that he adapted it from an earlier play written during his provincial wanderings—*Les Précieuses ridicules* (*Two Precious Maidens Ridiculed*), which twitted not the literary salon as founded by Mme de Rambouillet and Malherbe but its decline. The play made Molière a public name. (Death of Joseph Béjart.) Du Parc and his wife left the company to join the troupe at the Marais theater, but Molière acquired the services of two useful young men, La Grange (who became Molière's friend and wrote up many of the events in the company's life in his *Register*) and Du Croisy, and also a leading comedian, Jodelet, who died some months after the opening of *Les Précieuses ridicules*.

1660 — The Louvre underwent alterations, and Molière was forced to move to the Palais-Royal. His last opening at the Petit-Bourbon was a new comedy *Sganarelle, ou le Cocu imaginaire (Sganarelle, or the Imaginary Cuckold)*, which proved an even bigger hit than *Les Précieuses*. Both these plays were printed illegally by a man named Ribou. Molière took out an injunction against Ribou for *Les Précieuses*, but they came to an agreement for *Sganarelle*. (Publishing a play after its first run was tantamount to placing it in the public domain. A playwright might make a little money from the sales of the book, but he would lose performance royalties.) Molière resumed the royal sinecure of *tapissier ordinaire*, which he had renounced some years earlier.

1661 — A hard but productive year; he was now dividing his labors between public showings in Paris and private divertissements for the King and the Court at various chateaus. *Dom Garcie de Navarre (Don Garcia of Navarre, or The Jealous Prince)*, a heroic comedy, was Molière's first production at the Palais-Royal; it was withdrawn after seven performances and is still regarded as one of his weakest plays; in emulating the movements of tragedy it followed some of the more florid conventions of the time, and the motives of its characters are not made clear. *L'École des maris (The School for Husbands)*, another Paris production, contrasted the marital behavior of two brothers, one brutal, the other indulgent, and became highly successful. *Les Fâcheux (The Bores)* was a three-act comedy with ballet, music, and elaborate stage machinery and artifice, which was written and produced for the opening of Fouquet's chateau and estate at Vaux-le-Vicomte. (Fouquet was the royal superintendent of taxes; his self-aggrandizement in the construction and decoration of Vaux—to say nothing of his tactless advances to the King's mistress—led to his arrest three weeks afterward.) *Les Fâcheux*, which displays a gallery of public nuisances—people who brag, people who importune, people who talk endlessly—is one of the few examples of a play about bores which is not boring. Molière played several of the parts.

1662 — In February he married the nineteen-year-old Armande Béjart, who may have been Madeleine's sister or daughter and had spent at least a few of her young years traveling with the company. A number of ill-wishers claimed that she was Molière's own daughter; among them was Montfleury, an actor with the Hôtel de Bourgogne group, who wrote to Louis XIV questioning the royal protection of Molière. In December *L'École des Femmes* (*The School for Wives*) was played at the Palais-Royal, with Molière as Arnolphe the jealous guardian and Mlle de Brie, a charming comedienne, as his innocent ward Agnès. The play added fuel to a public controversy over whether Armande was cuckolding her husband. Two more actors, La Thorillière and Brécourt, joined the company.

1663 — Such violent criticism had been aroused by *The School for Wives* that Boileau wrote a public defense of it and Molière announced that he would reply to his detractors with another play. This was *La Critique de l'École des Femmes* (*The Criticism of The School for Wives*), produced in June. Certain noblemen were offended by this play, believing themselves pilloried in it; Molière is supposed to have received threatening letters and to have been manhandled in public. Several plays were written in response to *La Critique*, among them *Zélinde* by Donneau de Visé and *Le Portrait du Peintre* (*The Painter Painted*) by Boursault, this last to be offered by Molière's rivals at the Hôtel de Bourgogne on October 19. To beat this play on the boards Molière wrote and put together *L'Impromptu de Versailles* (*The Rehearsal at Versailles*) within a week; it appeared on October 18 at Versailles (built, interestingly enough, by Louis as a retort to Fouquet's edifice at Vaux), and was then transferred to Paris. This play in turn called forth more replies, such as De Visé's *The Marquess' Vengeance* and *The Rehearsal at the Hôtel de Condé* by the son of Montfleury the actor, who was now accusing Molière of, among other unpleasant habits, incest. Molière's rivals at the Hôtel de Bourgogne were not content with blackening his name; they also tried to steal his actors away, but none of the actors went. Louis gave Molière a pension of 1,000 livres.

1664 — In January his first child was born; to prove his friendship, the King stood as godfather at the christening of the boy, who was named Louis after him, but died ten months later. Less than two weeks after the child's birth Molière presented *Le Mariage forcé*

(*The Forced Marriage*), a one-act comedy with ballet interludes (in which the King danced and rapped a tambourine), staged in the Queen Mother's apartment; two weeks later it was given in public. On May 8, a grandiose spectacle called *The Pleasures of the Enchanted Island* was superproduced at Versailles; Moliére's contribution, entitled *La Princesse d'Élide,* was a framework for the event, in which he played a character named Moron. Four days later, also at Versailles, appeared the first version of *Tartuffe,* in three acts. The initial protests came before the play was over, from the Saint-Sacrament religious brotherhood. There followed an intemperate essay-letter by a curé named Roullé, in which Molière was stigmatized as "a demon dressed in flesh and clothed as a man . . . the most signal libertine that ever was." The monarch sided with Molière and allowed the play to be read in private, but banned a public performance in Paris. Molière, whose troupe was hungry for new material and could not afford to pass up a potential success, vainly pleaded for the ban to be lifted. The Saint-Sacrament campaign against *Tartuffe* was intensified. Molière produced Racine's first play, *La Thébaïde (The Theban Brothers)* — Brécourt and Du Croisy left the troupe — Gros-René died.

1665 — Molière's production of Racine's second play, *Alexander the Great,* was in its fourth performance when the tragedian allowed a rival staging to open at the Hôtel de Bourgogne. (Two years later he was to lure away Gros-René's widow, the lovely Mlle du Parc, to play the lead in his *Andromache.*) *Dom Juan, ou le Festin de Pierre,* a five-act play, opened in February and had a lively run through most of March. *Don Juan,* like *Tartuffe,* stirred up powerful opposition from churchmen who saw in it only profanity. In September came *L'Amour médecin (Love, the Doctor),* a three-act with music and ballet sequences; it was unveiled at Versailles and transferred to Paris after three performances. Louis took over from his brother the patronage of Molière's company, doubtless as a mark of trust and respect at a time when the playwright was encountering much public vilification.

1666 — After the birth of his first daughter, Esprit-Madeleine, Molière fell seriously ill with lung trouble (probably aggravated by overwork and anxiety) and went on a milk diet. He was also having difficulties with his wife, who was being romanced by several pursuers. Boileau tried to persuade him to drop his acting, and he did so for three months, in which time he separated from Armande and went to share a house with his friend Chapelle at Auteuil just outside Paris. For two years he had been working on an ambitious verse play, *The Misanthrope,* which was completed and staged by June; he reinforced its run by writing a short, three-act companion piece *Le Médecin malgré lui (The Doctor in Spite of Himself),* based in part on *The Flying Doctor.*

1667 — Molière softened many of the references that had given offense in *Tartuffe,* added a moral ending, gave it a new title *The Impostor,* gave Tartuffe a new name, Panulphe, and wrote to the King (who was in Flanders on the battlefield) asking for restitution of his rights to put it on. But in the absence of Louis the Archbishop of Paris forbade the production in his diocese. Over the winter Molière gave three more divertissements, *Mélicerte, The Comic Pastoral,* and *The Sicilian,* as part of a Festival of the Muses at Saint-Germain.

1668 — He was now seeing Armande only at the theater, and was becoming dangerously ill. Yet he still wrote actively, and during the course of the year opened two masterpieces—*Amphitryon,* three acts in a new, flexible verse form and using elaborate stage machinery, and *The Miser,* a five-act comedy—as well as a boisterous three-act, *George Dandin,* derived in part from *The Jealous Husband.*

1669 — *Tartuffe* finally opened for a public run in February under its original name and played to full houses until Easter. Molière published the text, together with a long, explanatory preface. His father died in February, almost penniless in spite of several loans from Molière. *Monsieur de Pourceaugnac,* a bright comedy-ballet, was played at Chambord in September and in Paris in November.

1670 — Two more comedy-ballets followed, *Les Amants magnifiques (The Magnificent Lovers,* from an idea suggested by the King) at Saint-Germain and *Le Bourgeois gentilhomme (The Middle-Class Nobleman)* at Chambord. Molière took on his acting roster a young man named Baron, whom he had discovered as a child-performer and who was to become the leading French actor of the late-seventeenth century.

1671 — More royal divertissements: a confection called *Psyché,* which brought together Lully the composer, Quinault the poet,

Molière, and Corneille, the latter completing the text in a thoroughly professional way when Molière found himself too busy with preparations for the production; a farcical three-act, *Les Fourberies de Scapin* (*The Swindles of Scapin*, inspired by a comedy of Terence); and *La Comtesse d'Escarbagnas* (*The Seductive Countess*).

1672 — In February, Madeleine Béjart died at the age of 54. Molière finished writing *Les Femmes savantes* (*The Learned Ladies*) in five acts and verse, and produced it at the Palais-Royal in March. Reconciled with his wife, Armande, he moved back to Paris and took up residence in the rue de Richelieu. A second son, Pierre, was born to them but died in September. In that same month Molière fell out with Lully, who, by pandering to the King even more effectively than Molière had managed to do, won sole rights over all royal productions.

1673 — Molière's last play, *Le Malade imaginaire* (*The Imaginary Invalid*) with music (by Charpentier in place of Lully) and dance, opened on February 10. Molière, now in a very weak state, was implored by Armande and Baron not to act in this play, but he replied that every performance he missed deprived the members of the troupe of their wages. In the role of Argan, a healthy man who imagines that he is suffering from all kinds of afflictions, Molière collapsed after the fourth performance, during which he underwent a convulsive attack on stage and appeared momentarily to recover. He was taken home after the curtain and died shortly of a broken blood vessel, before he could be shriven. For four days his body was refused burial. Armande pleaded with the King to intervene. On February 21, he was interred by night, without any formal ceremony, in St. Joseph's cemetery. A noisy crowd attended the burial. The Palais-Royal was immediately impounded by Lully and made a home for ballet and opera. Armande and La Grange thereupon moved the company to rue Guénégaud and affiliated them with the Marais troupe.

Some years later Louis united the Guénégaud actors with the rival Bourgogne company. The so-called Troupe du Roi of 1680 became the forerunners of the Comédie-Française, whose theater is now unofficially known as the House of Molière.

The exact grave in which Molière was buried has never been known. One hundred twenty years after his death some bones, thought to be his remains, were exhumed, together with some assumed to have been those of La Fontaine, and were transferred in state to the Père Lachaise Cemetery.

Armande later married another actor; Molière's daughter married but died childless.

MEDIEVAL AND TUDOR DRAMA
Twenty-four Plays
Edited and with introductions
by John Gassner

The rich tapestry of medieval belief, morality and manners shines through this comprehensive anthology of the twenty-four major plays that bridge the dramatic worlds of medieval and Tudor England. Here are the plays that paved the way to the Renaissance and Shakespeare. In John Gassner's extensively annotated collection, the plays regain their timeless appeal and display their truly international character and influence.

Medieval and Tudor Drama remains the indispensable chronicle of a dramatic heritage — the classical plays of Hrotsvitha, folk and ritual drama, the passion play, the great morality play *Everyman*, the Interlude, Tudor comedies *Ralph Roister Doister* and *Gammer Gurton's Needle*, and the most famous of Tudor tragedies *Gorboduc*. The texts have been modernized for today's readers and those composed in Latin have been translated into English.

paper • ISBN: 0-936839-84-8

THE MISANTHROPE

AND OTHER FRENCH CLASSICS
Edited by Eric Bentley

the **MISANTHROPE**
and other **FRENCH** classics

THE MISANTHROPE
Moliere
English Version by Richard Wilbur

PHAEDRA
Racine
English Version by Robert Lowell

THE CID
Corneille
English Version by James Schevill

FIGARO'S MARRIAGE
Beaumarchais
English version by Jacques Barzun

Edited by **ERIC BENTLEY**

" I would recommend Eric Bentley's collection to
all who really care for theater."

—Harold Clurman

paper • ISBN: 0-936839-19-8

ACTING IN RESTORATION COMEDY

Based on the BBC Master Class Series
By Simon Callow

The art of acting in Restoration Comedy, the buoyant, often bawdy romps which celebrated the reopening of the English theatres after Cromwell's dour reign, is the subject of Simon Callow's bold new investigation. There is cause again to celebrate as Callow, one of Britain's foremost actors, aims to restore the form to all its original voluptuous vigor. Callow shows the way to attain clarity and hilarity in some of the most delightful roles ever conceived for the theatre.

Simon Callow is the author of *Being an Actor* and *Charles Laughton: A Difficult Actor.* He has won critical acclaim for his performances in numerous productions including *Faust, The Relapse,* and *Titus Andronicus.*

paper • ISBN: 1-55783-119-X

TOUR DE FARCE

A New Series of Farce Through the Ages

Translated by Norman R. Shapiro

THE PREGNANT PAUSE
or LOVE'S LABOR LOST
by Georges Feydeau

paper • ISBN: 0-936839-58-9

A SLAP IN THE FARCE and
A MATTER OF WIFE AND DEATH
by Eugene Labiche

paper • ISBN: 0-936839-82-1

THE BRAZILIAN
by Henri Meilhac
and Ludovic Halèvy

paper • ISBN: 0-936839-59-7

THE ACTOR'S MOLIÈRE

A New Series of Translations for the Stage by

Albert Bermel

THE MISER and GEORGE DANDIN

ISBN: 0-936839-75-9

THE DOCTOR IN SPITE OF HIMSELF and THE BOURGEOIS GENTLEMAN

ISBN: 0-936839-77-5

SCAPIN and DON JUAN

ISBN: 0-936839-80-5

COMMEDIA IN PERFORMANCE SERIES

THE THREE CUCKOLDS
by Leon Katz
paper • ISBN: 0-936839-06-6

THE SON OF ARLECCHINO
by Leon Katz
paper • ISBN: 0-936839-07-4

CELESTINA
by Fernando do Rojas
Adapted by Eric Bentley
Translated by James Mabbe
paper • ISBN: 0-936839-01-5

THE BRUTE

AND OTHER FARCES
By Anton Chekhov
Edited by Eric Bentley

"INDISPENSABLE!"
— Robert Brustein
Director, Loeb Drama Center
Harvard University

The blustering, stuttering eloquence of Chekhov's unlikely heroes has endured to shape the voice of contemporary theater. This volume presents seven minor masterpieces:

THE HARMFULNESS OF TOBACCO
SWAN SONG
A MARRIAGE PROPOSAL
THE CELEBRATION
A WEDDING
SUMMER IN THE COUNTRY
THE BRUTE

paper • ISBN: 1-55783-004-5

STANISLAVSKI REVEALED
by Sonia Moore

Other than Stanislavski's own published work, the most widely read interpretation of his techniques remains Sonia

Moore's pioneering study, The Stanislavski System. Sonia Moore is on the frontier again now as she reveals the subtle tissue of ideas behind what Stanislavski regarded as his "major breakthrough," the Method of Physical Actions. Moore has devoted the last decade in her world-famous studio to an investigation of Stanislavski's final technique. The result is the first detailed discussion of Moore's own theory of psychophysical unity which she has based on her intensive practical meditation on Stanislavski's consummate conclusions about acting.

Demolishing the popular notion that his methods depend on private — self-centered — expression, Moore now reveals Stanislavski as the advocate of deliberate, controlled, conscious technique — internal and external at the same time — a technique that makes tremendous demands on actors but that rewards them with the priceless gift of creative life.

paper • ISBN: 1-55783-103-3

DIRECTING THE ACTION
by Charles Marowitz

Every actor and director who enters the orbit of this major work will find himself challenged to a deeper understanding of his art and propelled into further realms of exploration. Marowitz mediates on all the sacred precepts of theater practice including auditions, casting, design, rehearsal, actor psychology, dramaturgy and the text.

Directing the Action yields a revised liturgy for all those who would celebrate a theatrical passion on today's stage. But in order to be a disciple in this order, the theater artist must be poised toward piety and heresy at once. Not since Peter Brook's The Empty Space has a major director of such international stature confronted the ancient dilemmas of the stage with such a determined sense of opportunity and discovery.

"An energizing, uplifting work ... reading Marowitz on theater is like reading heroic fiction in an age without heroes."

—LOS ANGELES WEEKLY

"Consistently thought-provoking ... sure to be controversial."

—LIBRARY JOURNAL

paper • ISBN: 1-55783-072-X